JUDGING
CARRIAGE DRIVING

Also by Sallie Walrond
FUNDAMENTALS OF PRIVATE DRIVING (The British Driving Society)
BREAKING A HORSE TO HARNESS (J.A. Allen)
THE ENCYCLOPAEDIA OF CARRIAGE DRIVING (J.A. Allen)
LOOKING AT CARRIAGES (J.A. Allen)
YOUR PROBLEM HORSE (Swan Hill Press)
DRIVING A HARNESS HORSE (J.A. Allen)

JUDGING
CARRIAGE DRIVING

Sallie Walrond L.H.H.I.

J. A. Allen
London

British Library Cataloguing-in-Publication Data
A catalogue record for this book is available from the British Library

ISBN 0.85131.603.4

Published in Great Britain in 1994 by
J. A. Allen & Company Ltd.,
1 Lower Grosvenor Place,
Buckingham Palace Road,
London, SW1W 0EL.

Designed by Nancy Lawrence

Printed in Spain by Printeksa S.A.
Typeset in Hong Kong by Setrite Typesetters Ltd.

CONTENTS

LIST OF PLATES

ACKNOWLEDGEMENTS

Sallie Walrond would like to thank Caroline Burt, of J.A. Allen and Co. Ltd, for persuading her to write this book, her husband Bill, Elton Hayes, Diana Brownlie, Phyllis Candler, June Hales, Frank and Jean Kinsella, Peter and Anne Munt and Peter Nichols for their help with the text, and Jenny Dillon for typing the manuscript. Her thanks also go to Anne Grahame Johnstone for her ideas and excellent cartoons.

The author is grateful to the following owners and drivers for supplying or allowing the use of photographs of their outstanding turnouts, which have been carefully chosen to illustrate each chapter, being superb examples of their types; Martin and Sybil Atkinson, Peter and Joan Clarke, Janice Clough, Chas Cooling, Michael and Heather Dias, Jon and Christine Dick, Philip and Jennifer Dubois, Mark Gaskin, Michael Gould, Anne Grahame Johnstone, Nick Hever, John Horton, Brian and Chris King, Peggy King, Tessa Malcolm-Brown, Lara Mockridge, Peter Morin, George Mossman, Peter and Anne Munt, Sidney and Carol Murrell, Alan Noble, John Outen, Cora Pinnegar, Betty Powell, Tony and Gay Russell, Cynthia Sheerman, John, Eileen and David Snowdon, Alison Thornton-Kemsley and Bill Vine. Her thanks also go to the following photographers for their kind permission to use their photographs: Michael Dias B.V.M.S., M.R.C.V.S. (plate 6), Elton Hayes (cover photo and 1, 19, 27), Peter Higby (main cover photograph and 7, 29, 30), Sandy Hannan (14), Chris Hoelzer (5), the Horton family (15), Laurie Keightly (17), Tessa Malcolm-Brown (10), Dean G. Miller (3), Hamish Mitchell L.M.P.A. (8), Jim Moor (18), James Morrison A.B.I.P.P. (11), Stuart Newsham (9, 21, 25), Stan Phaneuf (4, 12), Anthony Reynolds L.B.I.P.P., L.M.P.A. (2, 24, 26), David Robertson Solo Photographics (28), Carien Schippers (13) Sue Stevens (23), M.B. Tansey (22) and Barbara Thomson (16).

PREFACE

This book has been written for people who are already competent Whips and fully aware of the intricacies of different types of harness and vehicles as well as the production of horses for the show ring. For this reason, many things that have already been explained in great detail in the author's previous books have not been repeated here. This volume has been written specifically to help to bridge the gap between carriage driving competitors and the judges of their sport. Although the judge is referred to as 'he' throughout the text, this is in no way meant as discrimination and is done merely to save constant repetition. There are, of course, as many distinguished female judges as there are male judges of driving classes at shows around the world.

INTRODUCTION

Interest in the sport of carriage driving has grown dramatically during the past 35 years. The demand for knowledgeable judges of horses, harness and carriages has increased because over two hundred shows now affiliate to The British Driving Society each year. Competitors are spoilt for choice and the number of shows holding activities for carriage drivers now results in inevitable date clashes. There are some shows which specialize entirely in driving. The BDS Annual Show, which is held in June at Smith's Lawn, Windsor, is the largest one-day driving show in the world. Four rings are filled with turnouts of every conceivable shape, size and type from early morning until late afternoon. This show has about a dozen or so judges working throughout the day to deal with between two and three hundred exhibitors.

In 1957, when the BDS was formed, very few shows held classes for private driving turnouts. Those which did, such as the Royal International Horse Show at the White City in London and the Royal Richmond Horse Show in Surrey, had entries that, in present terms, would be described as sparse. There were a few beautiful turnouts at the top of the line but a definite mediocrity towards the tail end.

The membership of the BDS grew rapidly under the enthusiastic leadership of the Founder President, Sanders Watney, and the hard-working secretariat of Bunny and Phyllis Candler. Many lovely old carriages were unearthed from the backs of barns and restored. Harness was discovered in trunks where it had probably lain, untouched, through two world wars, and was put to use again after the necessary repairs had been made. Horses and ponies were trained for harness work. Understandably,

1

1   The author and Major Tom Coombs judging the Private Driving Championship at the 1993 Royal Windsor Horse Show and awarding top honours to Mr and Mrs S. Murrell's Hackney Wentworth Prince Regent, driven by Mrs Chris Dick.

some members became anxious to show off their smart new turnouts. As the demand grew for more private driving classes to be held, the show committees gradually responded by putting on a class for these new enthusiasts. Shows were encouraged to affiliate to the BDS, who, in turn, helped by suggesting suitable judges. They also advertised the fixtures in their newsletters and journal. BDS rosettes were provided for all competitors so that no one went home empty-handed. BDS Area Commissioners assisted by suggesting suitable wording for the schedule and giving advice on the general administration of the class, such as the timing and size of ring required. They also advised as to the suitability or otherwise of the proposed route for what was then called the 'marathon'. This name was later changed to 'road drive' because of the confusion caused when horse driving trials became popular in the 1970s. On seeing the word 'marathon' alongside the details of the private driving class, some showing competitors imagined that they were going to have to take their precious, newly painted show carriage across rough country as in a present-day event when competitors drive their specially built marathon vehicles against the clock over all kinds of terrain, including water crossings.

1 · THE JUDGES' PANEL

In the early days of the BDS there were a few, extremely knowledgeable horsemen and women who had a lifetime's experience of harness horses and carriages. These people formed the original BDS panel of judges. Sadly, nearly all of these experts have now departed from this world, although, fortunately, not before they had begun to train and pass on their knowledge to some of our present-day judges.

Among today's judges are a number of people who have been driving for a great many years. Some have themselves produced and shown harness horses with success and therefore have first-hand knowledge of the procedure in the show ring and understand how to manage a class. Gradually, a panel of judges has been built up of respected Whips who are prepared to undertake the onerous task of judging harness horses in their various forms. The BDS also operates a probationer judges' scheme which is organized by the Judges' Selection Committee.

To become a probationer judge, a person has to be nominated by either an existing BDS judge or an Area Commissioner who considers that the Whip who wishes to become a judge has sufficient knowledge and experience to make a good one. References are then discussed by members of the Selection Committee who carefully consider the suitability of each applicant. Each probationer then has to attend five shows with five different panel judges in one season. Reports are written after each judging and are submitted to the Selection Committee for confidential discussion at the end of the summer. Those probationer judges who are generally considered to have adequate knowledge of the subject, as well as the ability to stage-manage the ring and handle competitors with the necessary tact and diplomacy, are invited to join the panel. Anyone who is considered not yet to have enough ability to cope with all that judging involves, is asked to fulfil a further year's training. Probationers are also expected to attend all judges' conferences and training days.

This method of training judges works well to keep the number of judges available topped up and to replace natural wastage caused by ill health and/or increasing age when some older judges can no longer face the nights away from home and the tiring journeys which judging so frequently demands. The work of a judge must never be underestimated.

2 · AN INVITATION TO JUDGE

It is most flattering to be invited to give an opinion which all of those who have entered the class presumably agree to accept when they make their entry.

Although judging is a matter of opinion, it is, nevertheless, very important that it is undertaken seriously, conscientiously and without bias. It is no good thinking that all that is needed is to read last week's show results in *Horse and Hound* and to follow the form book slavishly. Horses and ponies must be judged on how they are presented and how they go on the day. Like people, animals have their off days as well as days when everything seems to go right. Judges must judge what they see. Exhibitors put a tremendous amount of work and expense into producing a turnout and all are entitled to the same amount of scrutiny and consideration. It is unforgivable for a judge hardly to glance at a turnout that is obviously of a lower standard than all of the others. It has been known for a judge to spend the time when such a competitor is giving his or her individual show in chatting to the steward while he stands with his back to the unfortunate exhibitor. In actual fact, this Whip, who is going to be placed at the end of the line, is the very one who would benefit most from encouraging and constructive criticism from the judge to enable him or her to improve their turnout. Having to suffer the indignity of being ignored is likely to make such an exhibitor, who is probably a newcomer, feel that he never wants to bother with showing again.

When an invitation to judge arrives, either by letter or verbally, it is essential to confirm the exact date and which classes are to be judged, otherwise it is quite possible for a misunderstanding to arise and for the judge to discover, at a later date, that the

5

show secretary has put him down to judge a class for which he does not have the necessary experience, such as heavy horse turnouts when he is a light horse judge. I once found myself in such a situation and had no alternative but to judge the class. I was abroad at the time and the competitors had requested that I should judge them after I had finished with my light harness classes. Luckily, there were only three entries and the placings were obvious, so I emerged unscathed!

Once the invitation has been accepted, the judge is committed. If a more attractive invitation comes later, it has to be refused. I have turned down invitations to judge in America because of previous engagements to judge a small show in England on the same days. In fact, it does no harm in the long term because, if a show is really keen to have a particular judge, they will book that judge two, or even three, years in advance. It is important, when accepting, to confirm that necessary expenses will be paid, such as for travelling and overnight accommodation for the day prior to judging if the distance is too great to travel on the morning of the show. Some shows take block bookings for their judges at an hotel near to the show ground. If such an offer of accommodation is accepted, the show will usually pay for dinner, bed and breakfast for the judge who must pay any expenses incurred by a partner travelling with him. It is not fair to expect shows to pay for anyone accompanying the judge. Some shows cope with this potential problem by giving a set allowance towards overnight expenses, so that it is then up to the judge to make his own arrangements.

Contrary to common belief, judges do not get paid a fee for judging in Great Britain, although most shows provide meals for their judges and a friend throughout the day. It is essential to ensure that all entry tickets and a car pass have been received before setting off to the show. Officials at the gate at large shows are usually firmly instructed by the show secretary not to let in anyone who does not have the correct pass for the day, so who can blame them if, quite understandably, they bar the way to anyone who cannot produce a pass?

On one occasion, I was organizing a driving exhibition at a large, two-day country fair and had not been sent any car or entry passes. I had been assured, when I enquired, that all I had to do at the gate was to say that I was running the BDS display. I arrived at the gate in my car and the teenage girl on duty, complete with white armband marked 'official', had obviously heard it all before. People with a labrador had claimed to be part of the gun dog display and therefore need not pay to come into the fair. Another lot with a Jack Russell terrier were, they explained, to do with the terrier racing and therefore should get in free. Now, here was I, in a little saloon car, claiming to be running the carriage driving with neither a pony in the boot nor a cart on the roof rack. The conscientious young official was not, under any circumstances, going to let me into the fair without paying the required three pounds. My lengthy explanations about the fourteen horse boxes and sundry cars holding harness and towing carriages on trailers, which would soon be arriving, cut no ice. I realized that if I paid the three pounds, then the same would be expected from my display team, who, I feared, would take a dim view of this bad start to their day. By now, a line of cars had formed behind me, with drivers who were all anxious to get off the busy main road and into the park. My face grew redder as the teenager bellowed, at the top of her voice, to a man about 50 yards away, who was dealing with a similar queue of cars, 'D−a−a−a−a−d, she won't pay.' To my horror, D−a−d replied by waving his arms and pointing across the field into the distance, shouting, 'There's the exit', at the top of his even louder voice. At this point, Colonel Blank, the big chief of the fair, who had originally asked me to run the driving section, strode into view and saved the day. However, it was a salutory lesson which I shall never forget. No more do I accept that, 'It will be OK, just tell them on the gate and they will let you in.' I now insist that I have all the entry tickets for myself and whoever is accompanying me.

If the show is large, it is wise to study the map which will probably be sent with the passes and tickets. This will show where the judges are permitted to park their cars, which is likely to be well forward of the public car park. It is wise to keep away from the horse box area while walking from the car to the show area. Exhibitors, who suddenly become friends, may take this opportunity to chat to the judge, offering details of their most recent wins.

Leaving the car in a forward car park is a great help if the weather forecast has warned of such things as sunny intervals and heavy local thunder storms, making the decision of hat for wet or hat for dry, jacket for hot or raincoat for storms, shoes for dry grass or rubber boots for deep mud, easier if the car is not too far away for a quick change of clothes between the times of arriving and judging.

Such things as loos also need to be identified. Most large shows have superior, even luxurious, dressing rooms for officials and judges in the vice-president's or members' areas, which are set discreetly apart from the general public.

On arriving at the show ground, the judge should go straight to the secretary and report that he or she is on the ground. It is a great relief to the secretariat to know that the judge has actually arrived. There have been rare occasions when a judge has not turned up, due to a double booking, failure to allow enough time for the journey or underestimating the long queues which can be caused by thousands of people trying to get into a popular county show around mid-morning. It is for this reason that most judges arrive in time for breakfast at the show ground at large shows. A judge failing to turn up in time for their class throws the show organizers into a turmoil. A judge who behaves in this way is likely to be reported to the breed society or driving society in question and may even be struck off their judges' panel unless he can give a very good reason for his seemingly disgraceful behaviour.

3 · BEFORE JUDGING

It is a good idea to meet the stewards in plenty of time before the classes begin, in order to discuss the way in which they are going to be run. Experienced judges will have positive plans and the chief steward will be happy to act as required. I like to brief my stewards in advance so that they know exactly how I plan to run my classes.

It is vital to discuss the timing of the classes. For instance, if there are four sections which have to be completed within a certain time in the ring, it is a help to find out from the steward how many competitors have entered in each division. The timing can then be worked out accordingly so that more time is allowed for the greater number in one section than for the much smaller number in another. It must also be remembered that, of the number entered, there are likely to be some who do not come forward on the day, so allowance needs to be made for this eventuality. It is the judge's responsibility to be strict about timing and not to run over the time allowed in the ring. He can, however, ask the steward to keep an eye on the time and warn him when he has only ten minutes left for a section. Time must be allowed for the presentation of awards, especially if this involves someone like a sponsor presenting trophies. This can take a long time, owing to the inevitable posing for photographs and chatting to winners. Judges who wander around slowly, taking far too long to inspect each turnout or make up their minds, can cause a show to run late for the remainder of the day. This can disrupt the timing of the programme for the spectators and for all the other judges and competitors who follow on, so it is essential that each judge keeps strictly to the timing laid down in the programme. The only occasion when it is acceptable to run over time is when a message is sent from the show organizer requesting that time is wasted because the following display has been delayed and they need something going on in the ring to keep the spectators happy. I have, on such an occasion, been required to spend over half an hour judging one pair that was the only entry forward in the class. It was troublesome, to say the least. All that I could do was spend a very long time inspecting the horses, harness, carriage and appointments and then ask the Whip to go out and give a long individual show to entertain the spectators. The steward asked me to get up and drive myself but I refused because, for one reason, there was no actual need for me to drive as I was not trying to decide between two turnouts, which might have given me an excuse to drive both to see which I preferred. Secondly, I had knowledge that one of the horses, although appearing to be faultless, had been known, on a previous occasion, to kick through a dash board. I was certainly not going to risk getting the blame from all who were watching if the horse decided to repeat such a lapse of manners while I was driving it. Thoughts of litigation inevitably cross the mind at a time like that!

It is essential to read the schedule carefully, tear out the relevant pages and put them in a pocket. A judge must not look at the programme before judging and so must not be seen in the ring with the complete schedule because from the ringside this can look like a programme. The reason for this is that a judge is not meant to look beforehand to see who is entering the classes. In actual fact, through the season experienced judges will judge the same turnouts repeatedly all over the country and so reading the programme would not make the slightest difference to their judgement as they will already know who nearly all of the competitors are. However, justice must be seen to be done and looking at the programme is not allowed until after the judging is completed, when a marked programme is usually given to the judge to take home.

Having the page from the schedule in your pocket is a help when there are lots of special rosettes for varying breeds and types. It is best not to rely on the steward to get all these specials right. The poor chap has probably been stewarding for different judges all day long in a variety of classes, with everything from mountain and moorland to donkeys, and he really cannot be expected to remember every detail when he is getting tired.

It is best to be at the ringside about a quarter of an hour before judging is due to start. This gives you time to make a final check with the steward and to walk into the ring in a cool and confident manner. It is best if a woman judge does not take her handbag into the ring. It gets in the way and it is not fair to expect a male steward to have to hold her satchel during the entire time she is judging, while if she hangs it on a jump, it can get forgotten. It becomes the job of whoever has accompanied the lady judge to the show to be in charge of her handbag and sometimes her hat and gloves for rain if she has changed to hat and gloves for sun at the last minute.

Many years ago, I had one probationer judge who, on coming into the ring with me, remarked that she hoped that there was a loo on the road drive and added, 'I shouldn't have had that second gin and tonic.' In my opinion, it would probably have been better if she had not had the first one. Judging is an exacting task and needs a clear head. I pointed her in the direction of the nearest 'ladies' and carried on without her.

4 · THE CLASSIFICATION AND JUDGING PROCEDURE

Some of the smaller shows have just one class for private driving turnouts, when all the competitors, regardless of size and type, go in together. This makes the judge's job even more difficult as he is then expected to judge perhaps a Shetland pony put to a governess cart against a pair of high-couraged Hackneys put to a phaeton. Some shows which have put only one class in the schedule, add wording to the effect that the class will be divided at the discretion of the judge, depending on the entries forward. This, at least, gives the judge the opportunity of splitting the different turnouts into two sections. Very often this will be achieved by dividing the class at 13.2 or 14 hands. Sometimes a

Figure 1 A single with many faults.

class might be divided by type of vehicle if there are a number of exercise carts among the more traditional types. It all depends on the entries that are in the ring when the time comes to start judging. An open class cannot usually be divided until all of the competitors are in the ring because, until it is seen which turnouts are forward, it is not possible to divide the class fairly and sensibly to satisfy all concerned.

I usually tell my steward to ask the competitors to proceed at a walk on the right rein until the whole class is walking round. Then it can be divided as is thought fairest. Some shows state the divisions of the private driving classes in their schedule, so that competitors can enter whichever class applies to their turnout. The wording in the schedule might read:

Private driving classes for the best horse or pony, irrespective of size, correctly and smartly harnessed to a sound, suitable and well-maintained vehicle, suitable for a competent lady or gentleman to drive on the road. Commercial vehicles and Hackney show wagons are excluded. Class one: Hackney type, single, pair or tandem.

2 Martin Atkinson driving the consistently successful part-bred Welsh, Sparklers Masterpiece, to a spindle-back gig: winner of the supreme championship at the BDS show in 1993.

Class two: Non-Hackney type, single, 13.2 and under. Class three: Non-Hackney type, single, over 13.2. Class four: Non-Hackney type, pairs and tandems. There will be a road drive of approximately 9.5 km (6 miles). Special prize for the best junior whip. Special prize for the best turnout driven and owned by a person residing within 16 km (10 miles) of the show ground. Special for the best registered Mountain and Moorland pony. Special and reserve for the best turnouts in Classes One, Two, Three and Four.

The word 'type' is important because then unregistered Hackneys or animals with a dominance of Hackney blood should be entered in the Hackney type section. If such an animal appears in one of the non-Hackney type classes, and the judge thinks it should be put into the Hackney type section then he is quite at liberty to put the animal into whichever section he thinks is correct. The judge's decision is always final.

It has been known for an exhibitor to enter in a Hackney type section one week and a non-Hackney type class the following week. At one major show, I had reason to think that a particular animal was of the Hackney type. The driver assured me that his horse was part-bred Welsh. As it happened, on the road drive his ill-fitting collar rubbed the animal's shoulders to such an extent that he had pink patches when he came back. This, among other things, meant that he was placed last in his section. There were four entries in the Hackney types and eight in the non-Hackney section and so, in the end, the competitor settled for fourth place. I happened to meet him again, later in the day, and he then admitted that his horse probably could be called a Hackney type. There were no hard feelings. In my mind, this animal was a Hackney even though his papers may have got lost.

A scheme is now in practice whereby exhibitors who are qualifying for the end of season championships for the Sanders Watney Memorial Trophy, must state the type and breed of their animal so that once they are committed to a particular section this cannot be changed.

When the schedule has classes divided into sections, the competitors usually come into the ring in one section at a time because there would probably be too many entries to have them all in the ring together. Some shows, however, do put them all in together and have three or four judges working in separate areas of a very large ring or two separate rings. This can look

3 Jennifer Dubois driving the Hackney pony Bartholome Debonaire to a sailor waggon into reserve champion placing at Walnut Hill, USA.

very spectacular from the ringside and enables all of the driving competitors to be judged at the same time if all are going out on the road drive. If each section were to be seen by one judge before going out on the drive, some of the competitors would be kept waiting for a long time while the judge inspected 50 or so turnouts in their separate sections.

On one occasion, when I was judging in America, there were so many competitors in the class for single horses that the ring was entirely filled and there would almost certainly have been an accident if we had continued. My ringmaster ordered everyone to stand 'on the rail' (American terminology for around the edge of the arena) and, having ascertained that there was a duplicate set of ribbons and prizes available, she quickly and skilfully ordered the first half of the competitors, 'up to the grey', to leave the arena and wait outside in the collecting area. The remaining entries were ordered to walk on. Such were the good manners and discipline among these American competitors that no one attempted to jostle for position in order to avoid being left with a fellow exhibitor whom they would have preferred to avoid. I then treated these single horses as two separate classes, which was far better for all concerned. My job was made easier and twice as many competitors went home with prizes and ribbons.

On another trip to America, I stayed with the show organizers for a couple of days before the show at which I had been invited to judge. We were discussing the timing of the classes because there were so many entries that we were wondering how I was going to get through the day. On this occasion I was allowed to look at the lists of competitors as the names meant very little to me, being a judge from abroad. We simply divided all of the classes that looked as though they would be dangerously full, at random, into two equal halves in terms of numbers, according to the order in which the competitors had entered. Competitors were informed of the revised timings of the classes and everyone was happy. The day started earlier than had been originally planned and went on later. As everyone concerned was arriving on the evening before the show, there was no problem about altering the starting time as all were informed as soon as they had arrived and settled into their overnight accommodation.

When they are sent their numbers and passes, competitors will usually be informed of the time when they are due in the ring for their particular class. Most experienced exhibitors will be in the collecting ring well ahead of time. It is sometimes necessary for a steward to be sent to chase up the odd one or two who may have lost track of time and are unaware that they are due in the ring in a few minutes. It is very annoying for a judge if a competitor comes in after the judging of the class has begun. The judge is quite entitled to refuse to judge such a competitor.

In America, the discipline at the larger shows, and no doubt at most of the smaller shows, is such that if competitors are not standing by the ring entrance ready to come in on time, the gate is closed and no latecomers are allowed into the ring. An announcement is made over the loud speaker to the effect that 'the gate is now closed' and 'the class is in order' and that is that. There is no argument. Very often competitors enter by one gate and later exit from a different one to avoid confusion when one class follows another in quick succession.

The exact opposite happened on one of the Channel Islands where I had been invited to judge. The day dawned wet but the old saying of 'rain at seven, clear by eleven' was firmly believed by the exhibitors, who, I later found out, were all due to come to the show on the hoof. I was ready to start my judging on time, at about 10 a.m., but there was not a horse nor cart of any kind to be seen on the show ground. I began to wonder if, for some reason, there had, at the last minute, been a unanimous decision among the competitors not to 'accept my opinion'. I was reassured by my steward that they would all appear as soon as the rain stopped because they would be sheltering in the potato sheds to keep everything dry. This turned out to be correct. The rain stopped by eleven and the sun came out. Very soon a great number of lovely horses and ponies in shining harness, put to a variety of gleaming vehicles, appeared and we all had a very happy day.

It has been said that a judge of carriage driving classes needs the hide of a rhinoceros, the stamina of a camel, the eyes of a hawk, the speed of a gazelle and the memory of an elephant. The judge may walk into the ring with a serious job to do to pass judgement on the competitors but he must also remember that he is, in turn, being judged by the exhibitors and all the ringside experts. Many of these consider that they know far more about the subject than the judge. There will probably be only two people who are really pleased by the result at the end of the judging. One will be the winning exhibitor and the other will be the judge.

When all are of equal excellence, the result is merely a matter of opinion and the task is far from easy. Very often, the most difficult class to judge is one where there is no outstanding turnout, with all of the exhibits being of a fairly novice standard. The judge then has to choose between several indifferent animals put to mediocre vehicles and wearing a variety of ill-fitting harness, and has to decide which is the least bad of those before him. On such an occasion, if there are only three or four awards, some judges prefer to leave the remaining competitors in any order so that no one is placed last.

Once, a very long time ago, I gave only a first prize to the person whom I considered deserved the award and withheld all the other place awards as I did not consider that anyone was of a high enough standard to receive second, third and fourth prizes. I then gave a commemorative rosette to each of the competitors, explaining as I went down the line, my reasons for not awarding the rest of the place rosettes. Fortunately, no prize money or trophy was involved with these placings, so no one seemed to mind. They just all came equal second as far as they were concerned. The standard of turnout has risen so much during the past 30 years that this would be very unlikely to happen now. In fact, there is virtually no tail end to the classes, as the one at the end is just as likely to win a class the following week under a different judge.

Obviously, different judges have different senses of values. They also have varying methods of reaching their conclusions. I like to see the whole class walking round when they first come into the ring. In my opinion, an animal that will not walk is a pity. I like my harness horses to walk and find animals that constantly jog and fuss very tiring to drive. Also, having the turnouts walk round for a while gives me time to assess them. I like to see an animal walking with a long, regular, four-time stride, covering the ground with the minimum of fuss. The overall impression should be one of quiet elegance with a pleasant outline. The horse must fit the vehicle. The driver and passenger or groom should also be in proportion to the vehicle. Whips' and passengers' clothes should be pleasing to the eye.

After all of the horses have been given time to settle, so that those who are reluctant to walk have been given a reasonable chance, I tell my steward to ask the class to trot. I do not like to see horses being driven as though they are in a trotting race. Private driving competitors should look elegant and no one looks elegant if they are tearing round the ring as though racing against the clock. The horse or pony that eventually becomes the winner will probably be the one which, as soon as it came into the ring, almost said to the judge, 'Look at *me*'. Presence is vital for a show horse. Its outline must be correct. Ewe necks and hollow backs look very unattractive. I like to see a well-rounded outline, with the horse's head just in front of, or at, the perpendicular with his poll being the highest point. Animals that overbend are likely to pull hard and be unpleasant to drive. I do not like to see a vehicle being virtually pulled along by the reins with the traces slack. When an animal goes with its mouth open or head turned to one side, it usually means that it is pulling very hard, however much its driver is trying to pretend that it is not. Such a horse or pony would be very tiring to drive over a long distance. An animal with a long stride, which covers the ground with a minimum of effort, is ideal. Such a pace will be easier on the horse and will not shake up his joints nor wear out his shoes anything like as much as a short-striding horse which takes twice as many steps and hits the ground much harder with every hoof beat.

When the turnouts have trotted round the ring about three times, I like to see them going the other way and usually direct my steward to tell competitors to change the rein. This relatively simple operation can become a great muddle unless care is taken to direct the proceedings correctly. The change of rein must be executed in such a way that competitors are not being asked to turn at an acute angle. The change must begin after the competitor who is chosen as the first to begin the change has come round the short side of the ring. Competitors are then able to maintain their rhythm through half of a figure of eight. If there are a lot of competitors, it is wise to bring the class down to a walk for the change of rein and to trot again once all have changed direction, otherwise there is the danger of turnouts coming face to face in opposite directions at an extended trot, as each is doing their best to impress the judge as they go across the centre of the arena. In America, the ringmaster always brings the class to a walk before the order to 'Reverse' is given. When faced with a large class, it is actually a great help to have the competitors walk as they change the rein, as it gives time to clarify in one's mind how the placings are taking shape. The turnouts are then observed on the other rein. If there are pairs or teams in the class, this is essential so that both sides are seen.

I then like to bring the turnouts into the middle of the ring, in any order, so that I do not have to disappoint anyone later by altering their expected placing because of things that I could not see from a distance but which became obvious on close inspection. Exhibitors should be lined up facing the grandstand or the side of the ring where there are the most spectators. When lining up the competitors it is important to leave enough room at the front of the line for them to give their individual shows. Enough space also has to be left for the winners to be brought forward for the presentation of such awards as the championship and any specials which may be given by sponsors.

I frequently tell the steward to make it clear to the ringside spectators, through the commentator, that the class is being brought in in any order. If this is not announced, the ringside experts can become very agitated, being convinced that the judge *does* need his eyes tested.

I then ask each competitor to come forward to give an individual show. I like to see the turnout walk quietly forward out of line and then stand while I inspect the equipage. Horses which refuse to leave the line up or show signs of nappiness are noted. The horse should be presented as near to perfection as possible. If plaited, the plaits should be sewn so that the stitches cannot be seen, not fixed with elastic bands. If the mane is loose, it should lie neatly on one side. White socks should be gleaming and must have been well cleaned before having a little chalk added to make them look even whiter. Chalk put on white socks which have not been cleaned thoroughly beforehand shows lack of attention to detail. The feet and shoes should be in good condition. I always used to pick up a front foot in order to examine the shoe and foot as there is no doubt that the saying 'no foot no horse' applies more to harness horses than to any other equine, with all the road work that they are forced to do.

On one occasion in America I knew that I was going to be judging in the evening when the ruling was for all judges to wear evening dress. For the first time in my life I was going to be expected to judge horses while wearing a long dress. At the matinée performance, I decided that I had better start as I intended to go on and let the grooms pick up the horses' feet at this show. The first class of the afternoon was for unicorns. Among the entries there was a unicorn of very high-couraged horses which, at first sight, I had thought would be my winners. However, when they lined up for close inspection, I saw immediately that they had bad feet, with lumps missing and nail holes galore. I asked a groom, who was standing by the wheelers, to pick up a front foot so that I could look more closely. He looked horrified at the prospect and, when I insisted, the horse flatly refused to have his foot picked up. The groom became agitated and the resulting chaos was that all three animals pulled in opposite directions and the foot never did come off the ground. Obviously, no one had ever asked this horse to pick up his foot while he was put to a vehicle. It is usual, in America, for competitors to rein back after they have been individually inspected. This unicorn became so rooted to the ground after this escapade that the rein back was out of the question, which did nothing to help their chances of a high award in the final presentation of ribbons.

As a result of the trouble that can be caused by a horse that is reluctant to allow its foot to be picked up while put to, I now always ask the groom to pick up a front foot for me so that I can inspect the foot and shoe. I then walk right round the turnout, inspecting everything as I go. The harness must fit correctly and be clean and well cared for. The horses' make and shape should be as perfect as possible, in that bad conformation usually results in problems. Such things as straightness through the pasterns will probably cause additional concussion and such horses are, in general, more likely to move with a shorter stride than those with sloping pasterns. Animals with excessively short necks, large heads and thickness through their throats are less likely to be light in the hand. It is often hard to find a collar that will fit comfortably on such a neck and shoulders. Long-backed horses will probably cause headaches for owners trying to keep enough flesh on them, owing to the space between the last ribs and their hips. The perfect horse has probably never been born but the judge is looking for conformation that is as near to excellence as possible. Someone once remarked: 'Where do all these ugly horses come from when everyone's foals are said to be so beautiful?'

Lumps, bumps and blemishes that are unlikely to cause unsoundness are of less worry than any which look as though they may cause trouble. For instance, a splint that is high up under the knee will give far more cause for concern than a more obvious, well-formed one which is lower down and, apart from being unsightly, is unlikely to matter. Curby hocks and weakness through the hind legs do matter. The pulling power is very much generated from behind and lack of strength here can cause a lot of trouble. Windgalls are quite common in harness horses but are unlikely to cause problems even though they are unsightly. Horses with clean legs are preferable to those with embellishments, even if these are unlikely to cause unsoundness. Broken knees definitely do matter. Once a horse has been down on his knees, he is likely to go down again. A horse falling, when put to a two-wheeled vehicle, could have disastrous consequences as the driver and passenger could be hurled forward from the seat and thrown on to the road.

On one occasion, while I was judging at the Dublin Horse Show, one of the entries had a large hairless blemish on one brown knee. The driver had done his best to cover up the bare patch with a substance of the same colour as the surrounding hair. Unfortunately for him, the weather was not on his side and the rain which came down while he was in the arena caused the disguise to run down off the knee in a brown streak on to the white sock below. It was not necessary for me to say anything. I just looked long and hard at the knee and sock and then smiled up at the driver who, knowing what I had seen, smiled back. Very often, it is not necessary actually to touch the horse's legs as most things can be seen without handling.

I used to lift the lips at the corners of the horses' mouths, to get an idea of their age. In this manner, it is so simple to see, at a glance, whether the horse is a youngster or aged. Someone then remarked that this method was likely to spread infection from one animal to another, right down the line. Now, I ask the Whip or groom the age of the animal and I believe that the reply is usually truthful, give or take a year or so. If an animal, which the driver says is four, looks younger than that, I do check to see that it is not two or three because, in Great Britain, such animals are not allowed to be shown. If the horse turns out to be under four then it must be sent out of the ring. The judge has to use his discretion over this, however, because, early in the season, a genuine four-year-old may still have a three-year-old mouth if it has been a late foal, so the explanation that the horse is 'four this time' will have to be believed.

It is important to check behind the blinkers. On one occasion, when I did this, to my horror I found an empty socket where I had expected to see an eye!

As the horse is being inspected, so too is the harness. Some of the most common faults found in harness are twisted curb chains, ill-fitting collars, incorrectly adjusted breechings and saddles that are put on too far forward and often do not fit correctly because the tree is the wrong width for the animal's back. Many people tend to put the saddle on their horse in the position in which the front of a riding saddle would lie, instead of sliding it back into the place where a stable roller would sit. Many modern driving saddles are not sufficiently padded and actually press down on the horse's back. Some have the crupper back strap dee bent downwards in such a way that the bend in the back strap presses down on to the horse's spine. I once discovered a tin tack protruding downwards toward the horse's back when I tried to get my finger between the saddle and the horse! Ill-fitting collars are almost as common as saddles that do not fit. Horses are expected to pull a load when they are either being throttled by the bottom of their collar, which is too short, or suffering too large a collar which rocks back and forth as they progress until it rubs them raw. Too deep a collar, with a visible triangle of light above the top of the neck when the horse is put into draught, is quite common, as is one which is too wide, showing daylight between the side of the neck and the lining. Breast collars being used with fixed trace hooks instead of a swingle tree is another fault often seen. Traces that are too long, so that the tugs lie forward from the tug stops when the horse is in draught, is another common fault. All of these things are noted when the harness is being inspected and an experienced judge will see any of these faults at a glance.

As he walks back towards the vehicle, he will note the Whip's dress and his position on the box. He or she should be neatly and correctly turned out in dress that is appropriate to the vehicle. An apron or rug should be worn to protect the clothes from dirt. Hat and gloves must be worn. The whip should be held in the hand and must be of a suitable type for the turnout. An upright figure, sitting on a sloping box with the feet firmly against the floor or foot rest, presents a far better overall picture than someone sitting sloppily with their feet tucked back underneath the seat. The colour of the dress, hat and apron should complement that of the vehicle and horse.

The lamps will be seen. These should have their candles lit and then blown out unless, of course, the lamps use oil. It is quite a good idea to keep a box of matches in the offside lamp, in theory ready for use. In practice, no one in their right mind would be stupid enough to drive out on a public road under two candle-power lamps as they would almost ·surely get hit from behind by a modern, fast moving car whose driver did not expect to come up behind a poorly lighted vehicle moving at about 9.5 kmph (6 mph) on a dark night.

The vehicle is inspected for suitability, fit, condition and cleanliness. The paint finish and lining are observed. There are now some very fine modern vehicles which are being built to traditional designs. It is almost impossible to tell the difference between some of those that were built at the end of the nineteenth century and those constructed at the end of the twentieth century. There is no reason why either should be preferred purely on the grounds of age, providing that both are presented to the same degree of excellence. The names on century-old hub caps do not necessarily relate to the maker of the carriage on to which they have been put. I once had a vehicle which, according to one hub cap, was made in Norwich and, according to the other, was made in London. Hub caps often get changed when vehicles are sold.

Private driving turnouts are required to carry spares. Some grooms and owners take tremendous trouble to exhibit a beautifully put together box containing a knife, leather punch, boot lace, spare trace, rein and hame strap, shoes, hammer and nails and all kinds of useful items, while other competitors, when asked for their spares, delve under the seat and produce a supermarket carrier bag containing a mouldy trace and a hame strap with a green buckle. On one occasion, when I was inspecting the spares kit of a competitor's team, I unrolled the beautifully polished trace to check that it was of the correct length to be used if needed and discovered that the harness maker had forgotten to punch any holes at the hame tug buckle end. The competitor was horrified when I held it up for him to see.

Although this inspection of a turnout sounds as though it must take a very long time, in fact it takes under a minute for an experienced judge to walk round and see all of the things mentioned above.

Once the competitor has been inspected, the groom can mount and the turnout will give its individual show. The judge will have told the steward what is required and he, in turn, should have told the competitor. It is usual for the exhibitor to be asked to walk forward and then to trot away from the judge for 100 m (100 yd) or so before turning to trot back towards the judge. During this time, I watch the horse from behind to see whether or not he moves wide or close. Then, as he comes back towards me, I check to see if he is straight or whether he plaits or dishes. The turnout will then halt before reining back. The horse must step calmly forward after reining back and then halt and keep still while the Whip salutes the judge. The turnout is then driven back behind the other competitors and forward into line in the place which it left at the beginning of his show. He then waits while the other competitors do the same thing. Throughout all of this, I am looking for a calm, obedient, well-mannered and yet showy animal which I would feel proud to own and drive.

If the weather is cold or wet, it is quite in order for the groom to put a quarter sheet over the horse to prevent him from getting chilled while the other competitors are giving their individual shows. Of course, if the judge should walk across to glance at the horse, the rug must be taken off immediately.

When all of the turnouts have been inspected and have completed their individual shows, they are sent out together to trot round the ring for a final assessment. They are then brought in in order of preference. If the class has been divided, it is best to send one section out at a time, bringing in each section in its final order of placing before sending the next section out. The turnouts are lined up facing the grandstand so that the awards will be presented from left to right as they are seen by the spectators facing them. It is again important to ask the steward to brief the commentator so that he can make it absolutely clear to those watching that the class has been divided. This is very important, otherwise the winner of another section can look as though they have been placed a long way down the line. For this reason, it is also a good idea to leave a large gap, if space permits, between the last placed of one section and the winner of the next section as it is then much more obvious to the spectators that there is more than one section. Another thing that I sometimes do, in order to make things clear to the grandstand, is to present a set of rosettes to a class that is placed on the right-hand side before I present rosettes to a class on the left, even though they went out first and came in again before the right-hand section. It is so important to remember to stage-manage the arena at all times, so that those watching from the side are kept informed and not bored or mystified by what is happening.

Sometimes there is a special prize for the best local turnout, which is usually very popular among the local friends of the people concerned. If there are local exhibitors from different sections of a divided class, then the highest placed from each section must be sent round the ring in order to compare them on their own, and this is greatly enjoyed by those involved. They can then be brought in, in order of preference, to stand in front of the line up. The same can apply to such specials as those for junior Whips or awards for mountain and moorland.

Then, there is often a prize for the champion and reserve

champion turnout. For this, the first and second must be sent out from each section as it is quite possible that the champion and the reserve may come from the same section as both are preferred to the winners of any of the other sections. When the final decision has been made, the champion and the reserve are brought forward in front of the other specials so that, in the end, the champion is the turnout which is furthest forward in front of the grandstand, with the reserve just behind, followed by the runners up and the locals and any other specials. Sometimes, the class sponsors or other important people come into the ring to present the awards. Throughout the presentations, it is essential that the judge makes certain that the steward has given the commentator the necessary information so that the public are kept fully informed.

Of course, sometimes it is neither practical nor possible to bring the turnouts forward in the manner described, in which case the awards are given in the line up, but this is not as spectacular for the onlookers.

When the awards are presented, it can be a help, particularly to novices, if the judge walks down the line and tactfully explains how improvements might be made. Most newcomers are extremely grateful to the judge for constructive criticism as long as it is delivered gently and with diplomacy. Most competitors love their horses and ponies dearly, so it is best not to say anything that may be hurtful about the animal if the remark is likely to be taken too literally. If asked later on how the animal might be improved by training then, of course, it is kind if help can be given. Some competitors occasionally show displeasure when they discover that they have not done as well as they had expected. They should realize that any display of bad manners is extremely foolish and will be remembered by both the judge and fellow competitors. Judges' decisions are final and will not be altered. The only people who may support a bad loser will be their immediate connections. An outburst will never be forgotten by those who witnessed such disagreeable behaviour. Extreme examples may be reported to the breed or driving societies and in some cases such people have had their membership terminated and been excluded from competing again at the show concerned.

After all the awards have been presented, the competitors leave the ring with the champion and reserve champion leading the way. There is something very satisfying in seeing the class leaving the ring in the order of the placings.

It is very important to know, and remember, your reasons for placings. On rare occasions, the telephone rings later on and a competitor, who has been judged the previous week, enquires the reason for their placing. Once, when I was asked by a lady why I had placed her sixth, I replied that the reason was that I had liked her horse so much more than those I had placed seventh, eighth, ninth and so on. This seemed to satisfy her and I heard no more.

I was once invited to speak at a judges' conference in America, where I had been asked to judge the following day. Next day, the judges who had attended the talk appeared in a group at the side of the ring, with their chairperson, in order to watch my every move and decision. Luckily for me, every class that came in had an outstanding winner, which could be seen clearly from the ringside, so there were no queries. All went smoothly for me until we came to the open class for pairs and tandems in the afternoon. This class turned out to be one which most judges would have found quite difficult. As the entries came in, my eyes went immediately to a fine pair of coaching type horses put to a lovely vehicle. They were immaculately turned out and seemed, at first glance, as if they would be hard to beat. Then I noticed that first one and then its pair started to pull away from the pole. The longer they remained in the ring, the worse they went so I had to change my ideas. Next I thought that perhaps a pair of upstanding chestnuts put to a high brake could win, until I realized that one of them was not going quite level. A tandem of Morgans looked good, then a lead trace came off. It was replaced but came off again, and again. This problem per- sisted. I then thought that the vehicle was perhaps a little small for the wheeler, although it was of very high quality. A nice pair of chestnut warmblood types were going well but were obviously very green. They were horses that would probably win in a year or so but were not ready yet. Their vehicle and harness left quite a lot to be desired. I was left with a pair of Morgans which, although different in height, went extremely well and were superbly turned out in good harness and put to a pretty carriage being driven by a neatly turned out Whip. These ended up as my winners. The rosettes were awarded and as I walked from the ring, which I usually did between classes, I was called across to the group of ringside judges to explain my reasons for these placings. They just could not understand how I had reached my decisions as plenty that I had seen from the centre of the ring had not been visible from the side. I explained, in far greater detail than I have here, why I had placed each turnout in the particular order and there was then no doubt in anyone's mind that what I had done was right. Their chairperson then followed on by telling her group how important it is to have good reasons for particular placings so that, in such an eventuality as this class, the judge, at least, is convinced that he has given the right verdict and will stand by what he has done with positive feelings. A judge must be confident that his decision is the right one.

At this particular show, I went into the ring at about 8.30 a.m. and finally walked out at about 5.30 p.m., having had only the odd five-minute break between classes. There were so many entries that the organizer decided to divide any class which was too full to handle in comfort. The result was a very long judging day but, as far as I was concerned, preferable to being faced with several huge classes, one after another, which I would have found more tiring. It was purely coincidental that almost every class had a clear winner, which left the ringside experts satisfied with this visiting judge from England. A temperature in the high eighties necessitated the wearing of dark glasses and a wide-brimmed sun hat, so I began the day in this manner in order to remain consistent throughout. Lack of eye and head protection would probably have resulted in the lack of a judge once the height of the sun was felt on my eyes and the back of my neck.

A tremendous number of similar bay and chestnut Morgan horses were entered, driven to such vehicles as Meadowbrooks, and sometimes the same horse was put to a different vehicle, with a different driver, to appear later in the day in another class. It was interesting to note how consistent some of these fine animals were in coming forward to win again, being judged each time on the performance given. The ringside judges did not realize that one such animal was, in fact, the same horse that had won a class in the morning until I told them. A competitor sometimes thinks that a judge has 'missed' them and 'got lost' when they have won a class in the morning and been put down the line later in the day. It is perhaps a good plan,

4 Philip Dubois and his Morgan stallion Otter Brook Galahad put to a Meadowbrook cart. Winners of many types of class in the USA.

depending on the circumstances and the person, to mention to the driver, when giving a lower award, the reason for doing so, in order to make the exhibitor realize that the judge has not missed the horse. Like people, animals get tired and some can lose their sparkle when they begin to get weary.

One competitor, an irate 'county' lady, accosted the bowler-hatted, very English, gentleman judge after a class at a large show in Great Britain with the comment: 'I don't understand. Earlier this season you placed me first at the County Show, last week you put me top at the Blankshire but today you obviously did not recognize me.'

The judge took off his bowler hat, gave a deep bow and said, with charm, 'Madam, you surely don't expect me to make the same mistake *three* times.'

5 · THE ROAD DRIVE

With a private driving class there is quite often a road drive. This is not a race, nor is it judged on time in any way. It is merely to enable the judge to see how the horses go on the road. It is usual for competitors to be inspected and any divisions of the class made before the competitors go out on the road. The inspection is necessary in the interests of safety. There are occasions when a competitor has to be stopped from going on the drive because the turnout is not safe. There was once a case where the harness was so bad that I feared an accident might result if I allowed the turnout to go out on the road in convoy. After all the turnouts have been seen by the judge, it is usual for him to be taken ahead, in a car, by a steward to a strategic point from where he can watch all the competitors as they drive by. The drive is likely to be led by a show official in a marked car with a flashing light, or by a police car or motor cycle. Road junctions and crossings are usually policed or stewarded, again in the interests of safety.

The speed of the road drive is quite gentle, about 9.5 kmph (6 mph). The judge will be looking for animals that are giving their drivers and passengers a pleasant drive without any fuss or bother. Horses that pull hard or are difficult will be noted. Once all the exhibitors have gone by, the steward usually takes the judge on a short cut across the route, in order to come out ahead of the competitors again and the procedure is then repeated. When the turnouts return to the showground, they make their way towards the ring and sometimes have to wait for a while until the ring is free. This gives the judge a chance to have another look at the exhibitors. When the competitors go into the ring, they usually trot round a few times to enable the spectators to see some action before they are brought into the centre, facing the grandstand, in their sections. If time permits, individual shows are given before the awards are presented after the turnouts have been placed in the desired order, as explained previously. Procedures vary from one show to another according to the time devoted to the particular class.

Sometimes a judge will make his final decision after driving some, or all, of the exhibits. The problem with this nowadays is that if there were to be an accident, litigation could prove very expensive.

6 · THE EXERCISE CART CLASS

The main purpose of the exercise cart class is to give people who do not have a traditionally styled vehicle an opportunity to compete. Sometimes the class is restricted to novice Whips driving novice animals, so that the class really is limited to beginners. Usually these newcomers to the sport of driving have not yet invested the large amount of money that is needed these days for purchasing a vehicle such as a gig or dog cart in show condition. Perhaps they want to be sure, before spending a lot of money, that they really are interested in showing a harness horse and are prepared to commit themselves, and possibly their family, to all the work entailed. Some exercise cart classes are open to allcomers. This is then a useful class which enables the experienced driver to produce a young animal in what he hopes will be quiet surroundings. The judge has many considerations when he looks at the vehicles in this class. It has been known for an exhibitor to come into the exercise cart class in a traditional country cart with the reasoning that, 'I always use this for exercising'. The judge will probably not welcome such an exhibitor in the class and he would be quite entitled to ask him to leave the ring or, if he would prefer, to stand at the end of the line.

Exercise carts come in all shapes and sizes, from very low and sometimes badly balanced vehicles on pneumatic tyres to the superb examples that are now being produced for use at horse driving trials. The cheapest examples have various drawbacks such as the lack of rear or side rails to the seats. This is extremely dangerous as it is quite possible for the driver and passenger to be catapulted off the back or side and end up on the road. Lack of seat straps can have the same effect if the cushion is left loose

5   Lara Mockridge having just won an exercise cart class with Romany Lee to a Bennington buggy.

on the seat, which is another common practice among novices.

Some exercise carts can be very difficult to mount as this entails climbing over rails in order to get into the back of the vehicle. It is even worse trying to get out in a hurry and is, in my opinion, a dangerous state of affairs. This is where the slang term 'trap' originated. Being trapped in a vehicle is not a lot of fun if the motive power is being troublesome! Carts on very small wheels have a disadvantage in that the forward vision of the Whip can be blocked by the horse's hind quarters. Small-wheeled vehicles are also much harder for the animal to pull as coming out of every pothole needs more pulling power than for those carts with large wheels, which ride over the top of such dips in the surface. Carts with small wheels are also often more difficult to balance when going up and down hills in that they tend to ride shaft light or shaft heavy depending on the gradient.

Some of the cross-country vehicles now being built to a very high standard by numerous manufacturers are those that are likely to be most favoured by the judge. They are usually constructed with metal frames, tubular metal shafts and on quite large metal wheels which are rubber-shod in clencher channels. Many of these two wheelers have a means of adjusting the balance by turning a handle at the rear of the vehicle to move the body backwards or forwards on runners. These carts often have a large rear step on which a groom can ride for the cross-country phase of an event. The balance is then adjusted as necessary when the groom wishes to sit beside the driver at other times, as for the dressage or cones phases at a horse driving trial.

Some drivers of young horses may prefer the groom to stand on the rear step when the turnout is at its first show at club level. If the animal should get excited, the groom can then dismount from the vehicle in a flash to give help as needed. Assuming that the vehicle is correctly balanced when the groom is standing on the rear step, when he gets off the step the weight of the vehicle will then be put on to the horse's back, which will probably be of help at a time like this.

In an exercise cart class, where the manners and obedience of the animal are of great importance, the judge would normally expect to see the groom or passenger carried on the seat alongside the driver. Any animal that shows signs of being unruly would probably be asked to leave the ring in the interests of the safety of the other competitors and those around the ringside. A loose horse with a cart attached to it can be, and has been, the cause of a fatal accident. Horses must be schooled as much as possible at home before they are brought before a judge in the show ring.

Not all exercise vehicles are constructed of metal. Some have varnished wood panels on the body, splash and dash boards. Others, although built to a non-traditional design, are coach painted.

If the vehicle has varnished wood panels, then either black or brown leather harness can be used. Webbing is acceptable now in an exercise cart class, as are buffalo hide and canvas, although it does not look as smart as highly polished leather.

A vehicle which is coach painted should be drawn by an animal in black leather harness, although, again, webbing is now acceptable. On no account should brown leather harness be used with painted, as opposed to varnished, vehicles.

The driver's and passenger's dress needs careful consideration as they must be neither overdressed nor sloppily turned out. Hat, gloves and apron are essential for the driver and hat and gloves for the groom. A social passenger wears an apron or rug; a groom does not. A top hat must never be worn with an exercise cart and a groom should not be in livery. A bowler hat, felt hat or cap are all quite acceptable for a man, depending on the rest of his clothes and the degree of smartness of his cart. A lady can wear a jacket and skirt or a trouser suit. Polished shoes look well. Trainers look terrible. The groom or passenger should be turned out in such a way that he or she is neat, tidy and does not unduly attract the judge's eye because of his or her clothes.

The horse needs to perform in the same way that he would in any other showing class. The judge will be looking for all the usual attributes that make the animal pleasant to drive. The horse will probably be required to give the same kind of individual show that he would if he were put to a vehicle such as a gig or dog cart. Good manners are essential. The judge is not meant to think, 'He is a novice, or young, I will forgive him this lapse in behaviour.'

The judge will adjudicate as he always does, by judging what he sees, not what he hopes or expects to see.

7 · THE GOVERNESS CART CLASS

The governess cart class is sometimes incorrectly called the governor's cart class. The judge is looking for a turnout that would have been appropriate for a governess at the turn of the nineteenth and twentieth centuries to take her young charges out in for a country drive. It is essential that the pony is of a suitable type. It must, of course, fit the vehicle so that the correct balance can be obtained with the Whip seated in the offside rear corner. The pony should be impeccably mannered. A governess held a position of great responsibility to her employers and once the rear door was shut and the children were encased in the vehicle, it was vital that the motive power was obedient and safe. It is extremely difficult, indeed almost impossible, to open a rear door while trying to control an unruly animal. The sideways seating and lack of purchase for the driver's feet make the whole equipage very dangerous if the animal misbehaves. The added responsibility of two or three children could turn what was meant to be a pleasurable drive into a nightmare if things started to go wrong, so the judge considers such matters when he is scrutinizing the competitors in the governess cart class. Flighty animals with extravagent action are not suitable candidates for this class, however showy they may appear to their owners who are probably able to cope with their way of going quite competently. They probably do not have to worry about the safety of someone else's children while driving this flashy creature.

Some governess carts are painted, in which case the pony should be wearing black harness. If the vehicle is varnished, then either brown leather or black is correct.

The rear door usually has a handle set low down on the

6 Heather Dias driving Chinese Chequer, winner of the governess cart class at the BDS show on eight occasions.

outside, which can only be reached by the long arm of an adult. This prevented small hands from mischievously opening the door from the inside while the governess was looking elsewhere. Some vehicles have a latch at the top of the door, which can then be opened by pushing this with an elbow, allowing the two hands to remain on the reins and the whip.

The whip holder is usually placed on the outside of the offside rear corner, so, before mounting from the off side, it is necessary to remove the whip, otherwise it gets in the way as the reins are brought round from the offside terret. Of course, this problem does not arise if mounting from the near side.

The body of the vehicle is usually constructed so that it lies between full elliptical springs on a cranked axle, in order to keep it low to the ground and make it less likely to turn over.

It is important that the driver and passengers are seated along the inward-facing bench seats in such a way that the governess cart balances correctly so that there is no weight on the pony's back nor on its girth area. For this reason, it is important that the children are not permitted to move about along the seat once the balance point is found. A dog, which is carried on the floor, can cause tremendous problems if it is allowed to wander backwards and forwards from one child to another.

8 · THE COUNTRY CART CLASS

As the title suggests, entries in the country cart class should be suitable for country driving. The overall impression given to the judge ·should be of a rustic nature, in preference to a turnout that would have been more suitable for town driving a century ago. Vehicles need to be of the dog cart, Ralli car and country cart variety, with either two or four wheels.

The animal should probably be of a cobby type suitable for country driving, rather than one that is extravagantly high-stepping. A cob wearing a set of highly polished brown harness, put to a varnished dog cart, is possibly the ideal candidate for first prize. Some people favour the use of a brown collar, with the rest of the harness being black, as is the tradition with road coaches. This gives a sporting look to the harness and is quite acceptable. The standard of these classes is now so high that the cob in question will need to be a really good free mover with a lot of presence and the vehicle will have to be a fine example of its type.

The dress of both Whip and passenger should match the country 'flavour' of the horse, vehicle and harness and be 'tweedy' rather than 'towny'. Top hats and frills are not suitable and will not please the judge in this class.

7 Anne Grahame Johnstone's Welsh cob Scole Cam, driven to a dog cart by Nick Peecock: winners of country cart classes at BDS shows.

9 · JUNIOR WHIPS

The junior Whip class is judged mainly on the way in which the young person drives. Obviously, the pony, vehicle, harness and junior must be turned out correctly, safely and neatly. The animal must be suitable for the Whip to drive but brilliance, or otherwise, of the horse or pony is not dominant in the judge's mind.

The class is usually restricted to single turnouts. This is to prevent overambitious parents and trainers from producing four-in-hand teams, unicorns and randems for their children to drive. Such tactics can put the judge in a predicament when he is faced with one junior in the class driving a team among all

Figure 2 A junior Whip in difficulty.

the others who are driving singles. I have, in the past, had to judge such a class. On that occasion, the team driver was outstanding but this might not necessarily be the case. It could be that some of the single-pony drivers are, in fact, driving extremely well but it is difficult to put one of them above a junior who is handling a team quite adequately because they are going very quietly. So, in order to judge like with like, the juniors are usually restricted to driving singles.

I was tempted, on one occasion, to produce one of my very talented pupils with a tandem in a class in which the schedule did not state that the entries had to be driving single turnouts. This particular pupil had been unbeaten in all of her junior Whip classes for several years and was extremely capable. I considered putting my tandem leader in front of her pony in the shafts to have some fun in the class, as she had been driving them very well at home. However, we decided that we would

8 David Snowdon, aged thirteen, after winning the Junior Whip Championship at the BDS Show in 1993 with his Shetland pony Peanuts to a Liverpool gig.

only make ourselves unpopular with the judge, the show organizer and the other competitors, so we decided not to compete. The pupil had, by then, almost outgrown the class anyway, so it was wiser to stay at home.

One junior Whip class gave me some problems as a judge. Among the competitors who came into the ring was a very mature teenager whom I had earlier placed first in a showing class. His well-bred animal had shown a lot of brilliance to win its class and had been shown competently by this Whip. When the class for the juniors first came into the ring, I thought that this boy would be placed first. Among the other competitors was a young girl who had obviously been very correctly trained and was concentrating extremely hard on doing all that she had been told about sitting up in the proper position and the handling of her reins and whip. I like to sit beside each junior when they give their individual show. By doing this, I can chat to them to try to help them to relax and can also closely scrutinize their rein handling without them realizing as I direct them round a figure of eight or whatever I choose that they should do. When I sat up beside the teenager and his quality animal, I discovered that he was holding his reins upside down in that he had the offside rein coming over his index finger and the nearside rein below his little finger. As such rein handling was going to cause him difficulties in the future in the art of carriage driving, when he would presumably wish to progress to multiples, I placed the girl, who was handling her reins so correctly, above him. This decision resulted in one set of parents later telling me exactly what they thought of me, which was not very polite; I heard nothing from the little girl's connections.

In my opinion, it is so much easier for someone to progress to an advanced level if they have had the correct grounding in traditional rein handling, which has been practised with success by many generations of coachmen. Having to alter bad faults in rein handling at a time when the driver is becoming ambitious to progress to a high level is extremely difficult for both the Whip and their trainer. Judges of a junior Whip class are, after all, looking for young people who are going to perpetuate the art of carriage driving in its correct and traditional form. They will, in turn, be the judges of the future.

Some judges ask juniors to drive a figure of eight with the reins held entirely in the left hand and the whip held out to the side in the right hand, as in such movements as one-handed circles in an advanced dressage test. The junior must be trained for this eventuality. The secret is to make sure that the reins are held level. The junior must be taught to keep an eye on the rein splices. This is one of many reasons why leather reins are so much better than webbing. The hand is then turned to put pressure on whichever rein is necessary for the incline. If more pressure is needed, then the hand is drawn towards the opposite hip, that is, towards the left hip to put more pressure on the right rein and vice versa.

One of the most common faults with inexperienced juniors is that they hold the reins with one in each hand as though they are riding. Another common fault is that they hold the reins in the left hand in the approved manner but the right hand, which holds the whip, is never put on to the reins in front of the left because of the common misunderstanding that correct driving is 'one handed'. The poor child goes into all manner of contortions to try to control the pony with just the left hand in order to get enough pressure on to a particular rein.

Another common fault occurs when the junior tells the pony to go forward but the pony takes no notice. The child then wriggles about on the seat, moving his or her legs just as though riding, in a desperate bid to persuade the pony to move. The pony may then get hit on the loins with the reins, which probably results in it going forward with a jerk. On being asked about this questionable 'aid', the answer is likely to be, 'It's what Daddy does'. Later, I do my best to speak to 'Daddy' on the subject, as tactfully as I am able. Clicking is another 'aid' which I prefer not to hear. One click sounds much like another and I do not like this aid to be used by juniors, or adults for that matter. I far prefer to hear a command such as, 'Bobby, walk on'. My theory is that if animals are trained to answer to a click then they may leap forward unexpectedly when someone else clicks to their animal and this could cause an accident.

The dress worn by juniors is important. They should look workmanlike. Gloves are essential. Those made of leather are preferable and probably the most comfortable. I once judged a junior who was wearing white lace gloves, poor child! It is as well to have a spare pair of string gloves in case the weather is wet. Girls look smart in a neat jacket and skirt with a plain blouse and polished shoes. Boys can wear either a suit and a bowler or a sports jacket and a cloth cap if the turnout is inclined towards the country flavour. Top hats do not look right on little boys. When they are being trained, it is important for boys to be taught to take off their hats when they are addressed by the judge. However small the boy, he must be taught to hold the reins and whip in his left hand while he takes off his bowler or cap with his right hand, perhaps at the end of his individual show as he smiles at the judge before going back into line. If he is later lucky enough to be presented with a prize or rosette, then reins, whip and hat somehow have to be held in the left hand in order to leave the right hand free to take the award or have his hand shaken by the judge. Throughout all of this, a competent adult will be standing at the pony's head to help as needed.

Some judges ask the junior to dismount, fold the reins up into the saddle terret, pat the pony and then unfold the reins and mount again. Whether this is done on the near side or the off side is a matter of individual preference. The main thing is that the passenger should dismount first and mount last and the junior should demonstrate the procedure with efficiency and

Figure 3 The bad loser.

confidence. It is important to train the junior to tuck the driving apron into their waist band before attempting to mount. This detail can get forgotten when practising at home without an apron. The resulting confusion caused by a nervous junior standing with his apron between his foot and the mounting step while trying to get into the vehicle can ruin any chance of trying to impress the judge.

I once asked a nine-year-old pupil of mine how she had got on in her junior Whip class as I had not been able to watch because I was occupied in another ring. She beamed so much that I thought, at first, that she must have won. She told me that she had come sixth and then went on to say that 'The judge told me that I dismounted and mounted the best of all the class.' I felt just as pleased as she did.

Judges sometimes ask each junior a few simple questions about the harness their pony is wearing, so youngsters should be prepared for this eventuality.

The most important thing of all is for a junior to be taught to be a good loser if he or she is not lucky enough to be placed as high up the line as expected. They must be told to smile, smile and still smile. They will endear themselves to everyone around them. No one will ever forget, least of all the judge, if he or she shows any sign of being a bad loser. The only sympathy will come from their close family. A judge will never forget any lapse of good manners from any competitor, whether an adult or a junior, whom he has ever judged. Fortunately, such people are few and far between but their names remain engraved on the memory for ever.

10 · THE RIDE AND DRIVE CLASS

Rules vary in different countries regarding the judging of a ride and drive class. Some rules state that the horse must be ridden by the driver. Others state that the rider must be in the vehicle, so this person could be either the groom or the social passenger. Other schedules keep the specification open so that anyone can ride the horse, therefore a competitor must read the schedule carefully before he makes his entry, so that he is fully aware of the conditions of the entry.

Obviously, different judges have varying methods of judging the ride and drive classes. The most usual is to have all the competitors in, as in a harness showing class, and to go through the normal procedure to arrive at the placings, as for a private driving class. The judge then makes notes and awards one point to the competitor whom he placed first, two points to the second and so on, right down the line to the last placing. I always do this myself in case my steward gets called away which would create a terrible problem when it came to making the final calculations. With a large class, it would be almost impossible to remember the exact positions of those entries towards the end of the line. After the driven section has been completed, the competitors are sent away to saddle up and come back for their animals to be judged as ridden horses or ponies. At some shows, the ridden section is judged before the driven division. At other shows, competitors are told to bring their saddles and bridles into the ring, in their vehicles, and change in the ring. Such practice is not usually favoured, however, because of the safety aspect and also because it is rather boring for the spectators as some people can take a very long time to remove the harness and get the horse ready to be ridden. It is

9 Alan Noble and Michael Gould's part Arab Portsdown Knight Errant, driven by Alan to a spider gig. This combination has won the ride and drive championship at the BDS show on five occasions.

for this reason that there is often another class, of a different type, or a lunch break, between the sections. If the entry is large and the class has been divided by height, then the change can take place while the second height is being judged. This works well and makes it even more important for the judge to record his class placings on paper. In the ridden section, the judge is looking for an animal who gives a good performance under saddle. It is surprising how different some animals look when their harness is replaced by a riding saddle and open bridle. The horses must show obedience at all gaits and particular attention is paid to transitions to canter on both reins. Quite a lot of harness ponies and horses are reluctant to strike off into canter correctly and quietly. Many have to be forced into this gait and, as a result, go off with a jerk and a hump instead of smoothly and comfortably. The ideal ride and drive horse must be just that. He should be as pleasant to ride as he is to drive and should not be just a driving animal who can be ridden in that he does not buck his rider off. Any tendency to bad manners will not be accepted for a high placing in the overall result. Lack of schooling under saddle is frequently revealed during the individual show which every animal will be asked to give. It is a common sight to see a horse cantering on the wrong leg during a figure of eight, with the rider blissfully unaware of the fact. During the individual show, the horse will probably be asked to trot a figure of eight, showing a lengthened stride across the diagonal. He will also be asked to canter a figure of eight and should show a simple change of leg, through walk or trot at the centre. Some overambitious riders ask for a flying change and fail, which looks very unsatisfactory as they then often proceed in a disunited canter because the animal has changed legs in front but not behind, Of course, if the animal is highly trained in ridden dressage and is ridden by a rider of the same standard, then a correctly executed flying change looks splendid and is a joy to watch. On the same principle, any lateral work that is correctly demonstrated will impress the judge but badly ridden work of this kind will do the opposite and can be tedious to watch as usually such a competitor stays out for too long giving his individual show. On such occasions the judge is quite entitled to ask them to stop. The individual show should finish with a square halt and a calm rein back before stepping forward into halt. A salute and smile before walking back into line finish the display.

When all of the competitors have given their individual show, they will be sent out to walk round before being brought in in order of placing. Points are given in the same way as for the harness section − one for first and so on right down to the end of the line. The competitor with the lowest total becomes the winner. Two competitors could have an equal total. Person A could have won the driving to gain one point and come second in the ridden section to gain two points, while person B could have come second in the driven section but won the ridden division, so that both A and B have three points each. Competitor A would then emerge as the winner because, as this takes place at a driving show, the highest-placed harness horse takes the honours.

11 · WORLD BREEDS

The world breeds class is interesting as it brings together such animals as Morgans from America, Haflingers from Austria, Friesians and Gelderlanders from the Netherlands and Fjords from Norway. The class is open to animals of breeds that originated outside the United Kingdom or Ireland.

The judge needs to have a wide knowledge of harness and vehicle traditions, which are all individual to the countries concerned, and he has to judge each equipage on its relative merits.

10   Tessa Malcolm-Brown's Morgan Monnington Descant, driven to an American gig by Valerie Beckum, winners of many world breeds classes at BDS shows.

There might be a Morgan put to a light, four-wheeled American buggy. This horse would be expected to wear light breast collar harness with such differences as wrap straps instead of Tilbury or open tugs. The crew holes of the traces might pass over the ends of whipple trees, being held in place by rat tails. The horse would, perhaps, be produced with one, two or even three long plaits at the head end of his mane, woven with tape to complement the colouring of the Whip's clothes.

A Haflinger might be turned out wearing a wide, and quite heavy, collar with red, part wood, hames. The saddle would also be of a much wider and heavier design than is usually seen in Great Britain on a light harness horse.

A Friesian could be put to a Friesian chaise, wearing breast collar harness with white rope traces and white reins which can look very spectacular against the black background of the horse's coat.

The combinations are endless and the class can be great fun to judge. However, the entries do not have to be turned out in harness nor put to a vehicle from their country of origin. They can be put to any vehicle that is suitable for their type and any type of harness is allowed.

12 · MOUNTAIN AND MOORLAND

Any of the nine breeds of British Isles native mountain and moorland ponies are usually eligible for this specialist class, which applies to Welsh Sections A, B, C and D, Highlands, Dales, Fells, Connemaras, New Forests, Dartmoors, Exmoors and Shetlands. Ponies have to be registered with their breed societies and it is usually a condition of entry that their number is stated on the entry form.

Some of the larger shows have separate classes for Welsh Cobs, Welsh As, Bs and Cs and Shetlands, so that they are then excluded from the mountain and moorland class. The separate breed shows frequently have a harness class for the driving enthusiasts among their members.

The judge of the private driving class does not necessarily have to be a breed specialist. He will judge the animal and the overall turnout on their suitability for private driving purposes in the same way that he judges any other exhibit in these classes. Good conformation will be considered in as much as any animal with poor conformation is unlikely to please the eye in any showing class or at any time for that matter.

It is usual for nearly all mountain and moorland animals to be shown with full manes, tails and feathers, although some people, particularly those with Connemaras, New Forest and Welsh Section Bs, prefer to show their ponies plaited and trimmed in harness classes. It is important to read the small print in the schedule, which will stipulate whether the rule of not plaiting applies to the private driving class. Of course, it is always applicable to all of the in-hand classes.

The problem mainly arises for people who want both to show their animals in hand, for which long manes, tails and feathers

11 Alison Thornton-Kemsley driving her Connemara pony Laxford Gentle Muff to a Battlesden cart. Frequent winners of mountain and moorland classes.

are left on, and also wish to show the same animal put to a smart vehicle such as a gig, for which they prefer to plait. Of course, if they are going to plait the mane then they must also trim the heels. The exhibitor has to decide where his priorities lie. In an open mountain and moorland driven class, the judge may have a preference for full manes rather than those that are plaited.

However, as there is always so much to judge in a harness class, the state of the mane, tail and heels, as long as they are tidy, will be likely to be of less priority than that of the harness, vehicle, driver, passenger and all that go to make the overall impression. I have, in fact, won open mountain and moorland and breed specialist driving classes with hogged Connemara ponies. On those occasions, the rules of the schedule did not state that hogging was not permitted and the judges did not appear to mind. I have also won such classes with Connemaras that have been plaited and had their heels trimmed. The judge's decisions over such details are likely to be flexible.

13 · THE UNITED STATES OF AMERICA PLEASURE DRIVING CLASSES

In America, classes that are known as 'pleasure driving' are usually divided into separate sections for horses and ponies. There are other divisions for pairs and tandems and for heights of novices as well as for animals driven by juniors.

The American Driving Society and The Carriage Association of America have things very well organized. After the competitors have entered the ring, they are usually told to proceed at working trot. This gives the animals a chance to settle before being asked by the judge, through the ringmaster, to work in slow trot. After a while, the competitors are told to trot on or show a strong trot. If any incident occurs which shows that an animal is unruly, the whole class is immediately brought to a halt and the offender is told to leave the ring. The class is then sent forward again. When the time comes to change the rein, known as 'to reverse', everyone is asked to come back to working trot before being told to walk. Once the direction has been changed, at walk, by all the competitors, the turnouts are again asked to show the three types of trot on command from the judge through the ringmaster. All the competitors are then brought back to walk and called into the centre of the arena to line up for the judge to inspect. After each turnout has been inspected, it is asked to rein back a few paces and then to walk forward again into line. A writer (or 'scribe' as he or she is called) shadows the judge throughout the class and writes down the scores as they are awarded. For a 'working' class, 70 per cent is given for performance, manners and way of going, 20 per cent for the condition and fit of the vehicle and harness and 10 per cent for neatness of attire. In order to reach a final conclusion, if there is any need to see some of the turnouts again, those concerned can be asked to

12 Jennifer Dubois driving Otter Brook Alida and Greene Acres Debbie to an Essex trap on one of their winning occasions in the USA.

execute a figure of eight or work round the arena again. Any remaining competitors who are not in consideration for awards are excused and told to leave the ring.

The ribbons are pinned in the reverse order of placing, so that, for example, the turnout that has been placed sixth is the first to receive its award. This turnout then leaves the arena. By this method, the winner becomes the last to leave the arena, which he then has entirely to himself, enabling him to show his horse to full advantage in what is called the 'victory pass'. Morgan horses, put to such vehicles as road carts, Meadowbrooks, East Williston carts and breaking carts, have dominated the classes on the occasions that I have been invited to judge in the eastern states, while ponies with Welsh and Hackney blood have been predominent in the small height sections. Along with the Morgans, Friesian horses seem to be popular in the western states of America.

At some shows, there are classes known as 'horsed carriage classes'. These are judged at the walk, slow and working trot and on their rein back. Animals are expected to stand quietly, without being held by a groom. Of the marks, 50 per cent are given for vehicle authenticity, 20 per cent for harness fit, condition and appropriateness, 10 per cent for the horse's manners at rest and in motion, its way of going, the rein back and also cleanliness, and 20 per cent for overall impression. These classes are sometimes divided into formal two wheelers, such as gigs; two-wheeled informal vehicles, such as Meadowbrooks and breaking carts; sporting, such as dog carts and shooting carts; four-wheeled informal vehicles, such as road carts; and four-wheeled formal, such as George IV phaetons. All of this gives the judge plenty of opportunity to spread the ribbons around.

There are also classes for turnout and in these the percentages given are 40 per cent for performance, manner and way of going, 30 per cent for the condition, fit and appropriateness of the harness and vehicle, 15 per cent for neatness and appropriateness of attire, and 15 per cent for overall impression. These turnout classes are divided into numerous vehicle types as well as varying height and type sections of animals.

As can be imagined from all this, it is essential that a visiting judge from Britain, who is not familiar with judging using percentages, should have a reliable scribe alongside him at all times. I have always been very fortunate and have been given absolute paragons to work with on all my visits to America.

Judges are expected to work very hard for the fee which is paid for judging in America. They have to judge numerous classes with very little chance of a break, At one large show, where I judged for four consecutive days, the matinée performance began in the ring at about 1 p.m. and went on until late afternoon. I then had to dash back to my motel in the chauffeur-driven car provided and barely had time to change from my lightweight dress and sun hat, suitable for the heat, into the long dress required to be worn by lady judges for the evening performance which finished at about 11 p.m. when the firework display began. It was all great fun, although exhausting.

At this show, there was a gazebo in the centre of the arena, which sheltered the judges from the sun while they took it in turns to go out and deal with their specific classes. At the beginning of the show, the judges were introduced to the ringside audience who cheered and whistled as each judge, in turn, went out from the gazebo to take a bow. An electric organ was skilfully played to add to the entertainment throughout the show. The scarlet-coated horn blower and ringmaster kept everyone in order and worked in the capacity of my steward. His horn blowing was superb. After each class was judged, he took down the results and then offered to pin the ribbons for me. I surprised him by saying that I preferred to do this myself so that I could have a word with the competitors.

Entries were frequently numerous and did not permit time for anyone to give individual shows but no one seemed to mind. With the enormous variety of classes in which they could compete during the four days, most competitors were kept very busy.

As well as the pleasure driving classes, other competitions are frequently arranged for driven horses. Some shows arrange for dressage tests to be driven and judged. They often have a cones course for those who enjoy such competitions. There is also the 'gambler's choice', which is very popular. In this, a course is set which gives a choice of obstacles of varying degrees of difficulty with appropriate points to be scored within the set time of two minutes. All kind of ideas are used to make the course both interesting to the spectators and fun for the competitors.

Shows in America which have all of these classes certainly keep the judges very busy.

14 · THE UNITED STATES CHAMPIONSHIP

On one occasion, I was invited to the eastern United States to be one of the three judges of a special and unusual pleasure driving championship organized by Frank and Jean Kinsella. The system was interesting as I had never experienced this type of judging before. It is not a common practice in the USA and so I was fortunate to be included in this event, which turned out to be most pleasurable for all involved.

Competitors were divided into sections of horses, ponies, pairs and tandems, for which each entry had had to qualify.

Each judge worked independently in a separate arena and judged whichever class came before them. Competitors were placed in order, right down the line, but were not told of their placings. The only two people who knew the result of each class in each arena were the judge in question and the scribe. When the judging of each class was completed, the competitors moved round to another ring to be judged again until every class had been judged independently by each of the three judges.

The results were then fed into a computer and the placings announced at the competitors' lunch party. This was one time when the three judges were probably just as anxious to hear the results as the competitors were. Trophies and rosettes were awarded. The system worked well and was a lot of fun for all concerned. It was personally pleasing for me to see the turnouts which I had chosen coming out at the top of the placings. After all, judging is purely someone's personal opinion and, had we not agreed, some extraordinary results might have come out of the computer.

13 Peter Morin and Jennifer Dubois with the Morgan mares Otter Brook Alida and Greene Acres Debbie in tandem to a Tomkins gig. Champions in the eastern United States.

15 · WESTERN AUSTRALIA

Judging abroad can vary enormously. I was invited to judge in Western Australia at one of the major shows which went on for about sixteen days, on some of which I had a few harness classes.

The arena was enormous and each day a different part would be set aside for the driving competitors while other equestrian activities, such as show jumping or ridden classes, took place in another area. My steward was a great expert in the positioning of absolutely straight-line fence posts. When needed, he set out light, pointed marker posts without hesitation as he walked along and the result was an unwavering line which competitors respected and kept to the correct side of.

On days when I was judging at the furthest end of the arena, I was taken to my designated area in a vintage car as it was considered much too far to expect me to walk, although I would not have minded.

As well as my steward, who kept everything and everyone in order, I had a mounted 'gofer' at my disposal. When, on one occasion, I needed another ribbon, it was a simple matter to ask this runner who cantered off at great speed and returned very quickly with the necessary award.

Classes were divided for height and type as well as for animals put to different types of carriages such as sulky turnouts, buggy turnouts and viceroy turnouts. In these, it was important that the harness and animal were suitable for the vehicle concerned. One competitor came before me in a set of gold-plated harness! There really was something for everyone, with horses, harness, vehicle, appointments and driver all being taken into consideration. The two-wheeled sulkies, as they are called, look like

14 John Horton driving his Hackney Ellmore Ballerina to a Malee runner sulky, having been judged as champion harness exhibit at the Osborne Park Agricultural Show in Western Australia.

gigs but all had significantly longer shafts than I am used to seeing in Great Britain on a show vehicle. I learned that long shafts are preferred so that, if the horse were to kick, he would be less likely to reach his driver, which, no doubt, is true.

Another common sight was the four-wheeled carriages called buggies. Many had just quarter or half lock, being built on the lines of some of the traditional American four wheelers. They have a perch undercarriage and transverse elliptical springs. Most of the horses were trained to step to one side to enable the driver to mount and then they would step across to the other side, without going forward, to enable the passenger to mount. It was very impressive to see a high-couraged animal behaving with such obedience.

Many of the four wheelers have hoods. When I was judging this show, I drove quite a number of the exhibits. I climbed into one of the hooded buggies, behind an ongoing Hackney, only to discover that it was like wearing blinkers because my side

15   John Horton with the Clydesdale Pascoe Vale Jackson, to a butcher's cart, winners of delivery vehicle classes in Western Australia.

vision was extremely limited. Fortunately, the horse was beautifully mannered, so all was well, but I did have to look carefully before I turned, in case another turnout was just out of my vision but on a collision course.

There are some superb Hackneys in Australia, combining substance with brilliant action and excellent manners. It was quite normal to see a junior Whip driving a Hackney stallion with ease and confidence.

There was one lovely horse which, on the first day, refused to settle so that I could not possibly place it up the line and had no alternative but to put it at the bottom. I spoke to the driver who assured me that he would 'get it right for tomorrow'. Tomorrow came and the horse in question was now so dull that I still could not consider it for the prizes. The show progressed but the horse never was 'got right'. The driving judge, like any other judge, must 'judge what he sees' not what he thinks that he would see if the animal were to go properly.

On most days, after judging, the judges were asked to go to the press conference box to talk about their day's work, whether they were cattle, sheep, horse or whatever experts. Things that were said there were then likely to be printed in the following day's papers or put out on TV. It was easy to find plenty of nice things to say about the exhibitors, so there were no problems for me.

16 · NEW ZEALAND

Driving classes at shows in New Zealand are divided initially by the heights of the horses and ponies entered. Then, within their height section, there are classes for turnout, conformation, paces and manners. Some shows have classes specially for Hackneys, where the entry of Hackney type animals warrants their own section. There are also classes for pairs and tandems as well as for juniors. Donkeys, too, have their own classes in the various types. There is also a division called 'maiden', which is for turnouts that have never won a first prize in harness at any show.

16 Chas Cooling driving his home-bred Hackney Burnham Park Guardsman to a tray-bodied gig, after being sashed as supreme champion harness horse or pony at the Canterbury Royal Show in New Zealand.

17 Brian King and his part Arabians Kumai King and King Elijah to an Alfriston sportsman, built by the driver, on their way to becoming reserve champions at an event in New Zealand.

One section, which is classified as 'journey' horse or pony, is, as the title suggests, for the judge to choose the kind of animal he would most like to drive if he had a long journey to make. Another unusual class in New Zealand is for the best 'family' pony in harness. It is necessary for the judge to take notes as each turnout comes forward to give an enterprising exhibition of the suitability of their particular entry to try to win the first prize. Such tactics as crawling between the horse's legs and putting a dog on the pony's back had this safety-conscious English judge very worried at times. Luckily all was well and there were no dramas. This great variety of classes gives everyone a chance of winning a prize of some kind and works well.

As each award is given, the judge ties a wide, coloured ribbon around the neck of the winning animal. By the end of the day, a successful exhibit will be seen to have its neck almost hidden by ribbons.

When I visited, I took a few tricoloured rosettes to present for dressage and cone driving. These were much coveted as a change from the normal ribbons which I, in turn, greatly admired.

17 · CONCOURS D'ELEGANCE

The concours d'elegance, which is sometimes incorrectly called the concourse or concours dee elegance, is popular with spectators and many competitors. As the title suggests, this class is judged entirely on the elegance of the turnout. It is usually judged by an artist and occasionally by a dignitary, such as the wife of the show president or some similarly important person. It is sometimes even judged by a radio or TV personality who has little or no knowledge of equestrian matters. Possibly the best judges, however, certainly as far as the competitors are concerned, are those taken from the membership list of The Society of

Figure 4   How not to win a concours d'elegance.

Equestrian Artists. The concours d'elegance should be judged from a distance and the winner is the entry that gives the artist judge the most elegant overall picture.

Some judges have definite preferences, such as a passion for dapple greys. On speaking to one such judge, after I had been fortunate enough to win the class, I discovered that she restored old rocking horses, which was one of the reasons why she chose my dappled grey pony. Some judges like flowing manes and tails, while others cannot stand loose hair of any kind and so are likely to choose an animal which is plaited, with a driver in a hair net. In fact, long hair hanging down over the shoulders, whether on a woman or, worse still, a man, can never create a picture of elegance. Some judges like high-stepping Hackneys, while others favour low-moving animals with Arab or Thoroughbred blood in their veins. Light four-wheeled carriages, such as phaetons or those from America, are often favoured as they can look very elegant behind the right kind of animal.

18 Janice Clough driving her Hackney stallion Grants Tutor to a spindle-back gig. Consistent winners of concours d'elegance classes.

In the concours d'elegance, it is usual to walk and trot in either direction round the ring before being called in, in order of preference. Individual shows are not given.

Sometimes the concours d'elegance is combined with a road drive, for example at the meet of The British Driving Society at the Royal Windsor Horse Show and at the BDS Show at Smith's Lawn. The judge is taken along the route in a car by a steward, enabling him to see the turnouts during the drive. Very often, for some reason, the convoy has to halt and during this time it is vital for the grooms in attendance to be aware that they are likely to be seen by the judge who will be much more impressed by a groom who is standing smartly in front of the horse, even if it is obviously resting, than by a slovenly attendant who is lounging against a shaft, chatting to the driver. Such an appearance is quite likely to result in that exhibitor being dismissed as inelegant. The same applies if a groom on a rear-facing seat sits badly, with his legs apart or his hat tipped on to the back of his head. The rear view of a turnout is as important as the front and side views.

Period costume is not permitted and neither is fancy dress. There is often a tendency for more feathers and veils to be worn than in a private driving class but it is a great mistake to become too frilly and fussy as this can detract from the overall appearance and does not necessarily look elegant. Some competitors spoil their turnouts with garish clothes in an effort to catch the judge's eye. Some have overdressed children sitting beside them on the passenger seat and this can be dangerous because, instead of having the help of a competent groom when it may be needed, they have, instead, the added liability of a tiny infant. Toy dogs (the live kind) are another accompaniment that can give more trouble than help.

The secret is to strive for pure elegance throughout the whole turnout. The horse needs to be well mannered as lack of obedience will soon render the turnout inelegant.

18 · LIGHT TRADE CLASSES

The trade turnout class is usually extremely popular with spectators. There are still quite a lot of us who are old enough to remember when such things as milk, bread, greengrocery and laundry were delivered daily by carts drawn by vanners in London and other cities.

The entries in light trade classes are sometimes divided into two sections. One division is for two-wheeled vehicles and the second class is for four-wheeled carts. Sometimes the four wheelers are drawn by a pair, as in the case of a hearse or a large delivery van which needs two horses. The judge is looking for all the same things that apply to a private driving animal as far as presentation is concerned.

The horse needs to be of a kind that could cope with working long days between the shafts, being able to remain sound and keep condition. He must have a sensible temperament as well as look attractive. The tradesmen were extremely proud and fond of their horses. Many of them favoured animals with extravagant action, so it is understandable why many of the present-day two-wheeled trade carts are drawn by horses which show Welsh and Hackney characteristics. When I was a child in London, our local greengrocer drove a very high-stepping Hackney and it worried me, even then at about the age of ten, that this pony always went with his head turned to one side, towards the pavement, because he pulled so hard. He always trotted very fast and I had to be quick to catch a glimpse of him as he flashed past our house on his way home to lunch. Amazingly, during the lunch break, he was left, unattended and untied, outside his owner's home, where he remained by the side of the pavement, his head buried in a nose bag containing chaff and the odd oat.

19 Nick Hever driving Hendre Prys to a butcher's cart. Winners of light trade classes.

It is no good, however, for a light trade animal to be very showy if he is not obedient. He is required to stand quietly, unheld, and to walk sensibly as well as to trot freely to cover the ground.

The judge expects to see harness that is suitable for light trade work. For instance, a pair of horses that would probably be suitable for a spider phaeton, wearing a set of park harness, do not suddenly become a winning trade turnout just because they are put to a four-wheeled commercial vehicle.

The harness which is worn by a light trade turnout animal is generally of a more substantial design than that used for private driving. These turnouts were used all day, six days a week. The harness had to withstand the strenuous treatment to which it was subjected in all weathers. In general, white metal furniture was favoured as it needed less cleaning, although now brass furniture is often seen with trade turnouts. Wilson snaffles were most commonly used for light trade turnouts but now many exhibitors favour Liverpool bits. It was quite usual for parts, such as the girth and belly band, to buckle only on the near side. Now, much of the harness buckles on both sides. The saddle is generally wider in the flaps and has a larger and more padded top than many of those that are used with private driving horses, owing to the weight of an unbalanced delivery cart having sometimes to be taken on the back. The cantle of the saddle is sometimes edged with a metal strip. This gave protection against damage when the saddle was taken off and put down carelessly by a tired delivery man unharnessing his horse at the end of a long day. The bottom keepers on the open tugs were often made from metal to prevent wear caused by continual rubbing against the shafts. The traces are sometimes sewn to a ring at the hames end and, when putting to, the necessary adjustment is made at the chain ends where the traces are hooked on to the vehicle trace hooks. It is rare to see breast collars being used, as nearly all trade carts have fixed trace hooks at the splinter bar or shafts.

The vehicle should be suitable for the purpose of the trade for which it is supposed to be used. A baker's, fishmonger's or butcher's cart is sometimes enclosed in order to protect the food from the weather and flies, the goods being reached by opening a door at the rear. A milk float is likely to have a churn and ladle for measuring out the required amount of milk to the customer. A butcher or baker might have a basket for carrying his goods to the house. A leather pouch, colloquially called a cash bag, for carrying money and an order book is sometimes worn across the shoulder, being suspended by a strap.

In the show ring, trade turnouts are not permitted to carry goods. The driver should wear clothes that are suitable for his trade. Butchers, bakers, dairy men and fishmongers often wear straw boaters for summer driving. Aprons with horizontal stripes are traditionally worn by butchers. Fishmongers usually wear aprons with vertical stripes. When the turnouts come into the ring, they first trot round in one direction and then change the rein and trot the other way. Animals that tear round as if they are in a trotting race, with their mouths open and jaws crossed, will not endear themselves to the judge. Some pull so much, and lean towards the centre of the ring, that their driver is forced to keep them out by hauling on the outside rein, which results in a neck bent permanently away from the direction of the turn. Such an animal will not be favoured.

Turnouts are then lined up in the centre of the ring for inspection before being asked to give an individual show. Some judges ask the driver and assistant to dismount and stand back, away from the horse, during their individual show. I ask the driver to do whatever he likes in order to demonstrate to me the suitability of his animal for the job in question. I like to see a horse walk in a regular four-time beat and be forward going but not hurried. The trot needs to be workmanlike and to cover the ground with little effort. Then, at the halt, if the driver chooses to dismount, I like to see the horse stand absolutely still while his master stands back, out of vision of the horse. I like to see the driver mount while the horse stands motionless. Very few achieve this which, under the stress and electric atmosphere of a big show, is not surprising. In the 1940s, it was quite normal for a horse to stand unattended while goods were being delivered at one house and then to walk forward quietly on command from the delivery man as he went to the next house. A shout of 'Whoa' then brought the horse to a stop where he waited for a further command. Such procedure continued for several hours throughout the day's work in London. A late-twentieth-century show judge would be nervous of asking for such a demonstration of training in a noisy show ground. If there were to be an accident, litigation could result. It is for this reason that I leave it entirely to the individual tradesman to do whatever he chooses during his individual show.

19 · THE COSTER CLASS

The coster class, like that for light trade turnouts, is extremely popular with spectators.

Generally speaking, the four-wheeled, flat trolleys are pulled by strong cobs. Welsh type stallions with an abundance of mane, tail and feather are greatly favoured by the competitors. When the trolley is loaded high with fruit, flowers and vegetables, it needs a strong animal. The businesses practised by costers are many and varied. Some of them sell goods such as horse or dog feed. They frequently have a board on the side of their cart, which states their name and trade.

Some coster carts run on pneumatic tyres, while others have iron-rimmed wheels. On looking at the vehicle, the judge considers its soundness as well as its fit relating to the animal between the shafts. He will inspect the decoration of the paint finish and the presentation of the goods on display.

Many costers carry a water bucket attached to the underneath of the rear of the cart, as well as a nose bag with feed such as chaff and oats for the horse's lunch. It is usual for a rug to be hung along the back of the seat, ready to go over the horse during the lunch break or any other time when the horse may be kept waiting. Such details are all taken into consideration by the judge.

It is usual for the driver, and any assistant who is with him, to wear a white overall. Some wear a buttonhole, such as a red carnation, to match the trim on the harness. A straw or felt hat or a cap is usually worn. Not many wear gloves.

The harness which the judge expects to see is of a slightly heavier and more ornate variety than that used for the light trade turnouts. The buckles are likely to be of the horse-shoe

20 A coster cart and cob with the appointments suitable for their class.

design throughout. The bit may be either a Wilson snaffle or a horse-shoe-cheeked, half-moon bit. Some use Liverpool bits. A white rope and webbing halter is worn under the bridle in case the horse needs to be tied up. During the latter years of World War Two, halters were worn by most of the trade horses so that, in the event of an air raid, the horse could be tied to the nearest solid object, for example a lamp-post, while the delivery man ran for cover in the nearest air raid shelter.

Harness made up from part-brown and part-black is favoured by some people. The collar, which is always of the full variety, is substantial, with a wide bearing surface, enabling the horse to haul its load as easily as possible. Sometimes there is white decorative stitching on the outer side of the edging of the collar. Coloured trimming is put on the edge of the saddle or on the saddle pad under the saddle. Kidney beaters and face drops are trimmed with the same matching coloured leather, as are the safes or trimming on the open tugs. Tilbury tugs are not used with coster carts because the shafts are in one unit, being fixed by a rod, or similar, to the front of the vehicle, and ride quite satisfactorily in open tugs. The chain-ended traces are fixed to solid hooks on the inner sides at the ends of the shafts.

The description of the individual show given by competitors

in the light trade turnout class also applies to the coster cart class. Again, I do not tell any driver to dismount and walk away from his turnout. I leave it for him to decide to do whatever he thinks fit to prove to me how suitable his horse is for the work which he asks it to do in the course of his trade.

The costers take a great pride in their horses and the importance of a judge going right down the line, taking equal trouble to inspect all of the competitors, applies as much to this class as to any other. There is always something nice that can be said to each one as their standard of turnout is usually very high. If there should be one, at the end of the line, whose presentation leaves quite a lot to be desired, there is sure to be something that can be commended.

One elderly and very knowledgeable judge, of the old school type, was surprised when the coster whom he had placed at the bottom of the line approached him after the class and said, 'Are you free next Saturday as I'm running a little show and I'd like you to do a bit of judging?'

Surprised, and flattered, the gentleman judge replied, 'Yes, indeed I am free and would be pleased to do some judging ... what class do you want me to judge?'

The coster replied, 'Home-made cakes and jam.'

20 · THE DISABLED DRIVERS' CLASS

The disabled driving section of the Riding for the Disabled Association has grown considerably over the past few years. There is now a great desire among some of these drivers and their able-bodied trainers to have the opportunity to attend shows and be judged in their own right.

Sometimes the disabled drivers' class is divided into two sections. The ambulant section is for disabled drivers who are able to sit on the box of a traditionally styled carriage. The non-ambulant division is for drivers who are in wheelchairs. For such a driver, there are many types of purpose-built vehicles from which to choose, which allow their wheelchair to be loaded up a rear ramp. The wheelchair is then clamped into position in the off side of the vehicle, enabling the occupant to feel safe and secure to drive the pony. The judge will look carefully at the pony, vehicle and harness for safety and will not judge any turnout which, in his opinion, is unsuitable in any way.

The class is judged primarily on the ability of the driver who may use reins with adjustable hand loops if he is unable, through disability, to drive in the traditional British style. A headcollar is worn under the bridle and some disabled drivers have their reins attached to this instead of to the bit.

The driver must be accompanied by an able-bodied experienced Whip who must have a pair of reins fixed to the pony's bit so that immediate control is achieved if the need arises. The AB's reins should appear obviously slacker than those of the disabled driver so that the judge is able to see who is driving the pony. He will be watching this carefully as it is a very common fault for the AB Whip to be tempted to take charge of the pony when it would be perfectly safe to allow the disabled driver to

21   Peggy King driving John Outen's Zebedee from a wheelchair in a Jackson carriage to win the class for disabled drivers at the BDS Show.

be in control of the turnout. There are occasions when the poor pony gets hauled in different directions by two sets of reins being pulled opposite ways by two people. Such practice will not be viewed kindly by the judge.

21 · DONKEYS

There are now some very well-trained donkeys, wearing good leather harness and put to excellent traditional carriages at shows that have donkey turnout classes. The Donkey Breed Society Show has a large variety of classes for driven donkeys. The criteria for judging donkey turnouts are the same as for horses and ponies. It is just as important that everything should fit correctly and be well presented. Some donkeys are shown unshod and this is quite acceptable providing that their feet are well cared for and in first class condition. A good driving donkey will be seen to trot so freely that it puts out its toe and covers the ground with little effort. He should be well mannered and obedient to the voice and should not need constant nagging in order to get him to move forward.

If a full collar is worn, it will be one that is split at the top. Ordinary full collars are usually too narrow to pass over the wide forehead of a donkey if they are going to fit the same animal's neck. Some drivers forget the importance of having a swingle tree on their vehicle when a breast collar is worn. Fixed trace hooks used with a breast collar cause a lot of misery. Donkeys that are unhappy tend to hump their backs, clamp down their tails and skuttle along. This outline will not please the judge who will be looking for a happy, willing and free-moving donkey to take the top award.

22 Mrs Cora Pinnegar with Cleeve Pantella, champion donkey, to a Dennett gig.

22 · PAIRS CLASSES

In referring to the judging of pairs, Sanders Watney always said that the perfect pair is 'one horse or pony twice'. In a few words, this sums up what the judge is looking for in the horse power of the turnout. Ideally, a pair should be of identical colouring and have the same markings. If one of a pair coming towards the judge has a white face and the other has only a star, they do not look well matched from that angle. Equally, if one has white legs and the other does not, they are not ideal. When judging a pair, it is often a good idea to stand as near to the vehicle as possible, to see what they look like from the driver's angle. It is sometimes quite surprising to see how much they differ from the rear view, both in height and in width. Some pairs, which look quite well matched from the side, turn out to be of different widths over their hind quarters and rib cages when viewed from behind. Animals which have similar conformation will look better than a pair in which one is long and the other close-coupled. Their action should match so that they are able to trot stride for stride. Animals which have a matching stride will be more likely to be able to work together efficiently than two whose strides are of different types. If one is a low-moving, long-striding daisy cutter and the other short-striding, picking its knees up and putting its feet down after taking short strides, they will not be very efficient in their work nor much pleasure to drive. The pair should work as one.

Often, it will be seen that one horse is doing far more work than its partner. The judge may have to make a choice between a perfectly matched pair, as far as colour and markings are concerned, and a pair whose colouring does not begin to match but whose stride and type are compatible. The judge's job is not an easy one when so many factors must be considered.

One of the most common faults to be found when judging pairs is that they pull away from the pole. This is a serious fault which, once established, is virtually impossible to correct. Such animals are unpleasant to drive and, because the habit usually worsens once it is confirmed, it needs to be viewed seriously. The animals lean away, with their pole straps and outer traces becoming tighter, to such an extent that close inspection under the hame tug frequently reveals signs of rubbing or, in extreme cases, raw areas. Leaning against the pole is another serious fault that is sometimes seen. It usually causes both animals to sweat heavily on their inner sides and this, too, can result in soreness. Of course, both of these serious faults prevent the horses from working together properly. The ideal pair should be seen to go into their collars with equal tension on all four traces.

Close inspection of the harness for fit, cleanliness and condition is the same as for singles. The bridles should have the nosebands buckled on the outer sides of both animals. Correct bits, such as Buxtons, elbow or fixed-cheek Liverpools should be used. A common fault, often practised by newcomers to pair work, is to put the reins onto the plain cheek position, using Liverpool bits with movable cheeks. Then, when the reins are pulled and the coupling reins tighten, the fronts of the rings of the bits press into the soft muzzles of both animals, causing pain. This frequently results in mouth and head problems as the horses become more and more bruised and uncomfortable.

Another common fault is wrongly buckled hame straps, in that they are put on incorrectly, with the points facing outwards instead of inwards as they should.

A fault which is also common is that the false martingale points are not passed round the collar and hames, as they should be, so that the point of the false martingale lies only through the kidney link. Very often this fault is caused, initially, by the harness maker who has made them too short to allow them to go right round the collar, where they should be, in order to hold the hames in place if the need should arise. There is a modern tendency to pass the pole straps round the collars, which is acceptable for the cross-country phase at a horse driving trial but not for private driving or coaching. The pole straps should go through the kidney link ring at the bottom of the hames. It is important that these traditions are kept up because, otherwise,

23 Betty Powell driving her full-brother, Welsh section B ponies Berberys Black Diamond and Berberys Black Pearl to a Fenix four-wheeled dog cart to become show champions.

they will become lost forever to future generations. Pads used with pairs are often seen to press down on the horses' spines because they are not of the correct width for the horses' backs. As with single turnouts, crupper back straps are sometimes seen to be pressing quite hard into the animals' back at the dee, which must cause a lot of bruising and discomfort.

Another common fault is that the tags at the ends of the running loop traces, where they are fixed to the roller bolts, are put on in such a way that they do not all face outwards as they should to enable the trace to be eased in order to release it from the roller bolt when taking it off. Occasionally, it will be noticed that the coupling and draught reins have been put on to the wrong sides, resulting in problems with one, or both, horse's headcarriage in that it is turned in or out too much and is not straight.

The height and length of the pole are sometimes questionable. Too short a pole may result in the horses looking dangerously near to the splinter bar or swingle trees when they are pulling up or reining back. The same applies if breeching is not worn when breast collars are used.

At a show in New Zealand, where I had been invited to judge the class for 'turnout', which is judged on presentation, there came in a superb pair of small grey ponies. They were immaculately presented, being sparkling white, and obviously many hours had been spent in shampooing and brushing. However, their breast collar harness, which was as clean and polished as the ponies, had neither false martingales nor breeching. I spoke to their driver about this and he replied to the effect that he had always driven them like this and there had never been any need for these extra items of harness which I was deeming necessary. I explained that the ponies must find it very difficult to hold the vehicle back off their hocks when going down hills and I was told that there were no hills where he drove. I placed the turnout down the line and, not surprisingly, I was very unpopular with this competitor. Later, there was a class for 'style and manners'. The same little white ponies came in, in the same harness. During their individual show, I asked each turnout to rein back a few paces. Needless to say, the game little pair did their best but failed completely to push their four-wheeled carriage backwards through the grass. Try as they might, all that happened was that their breast collars went up their necks as the pole remained still and the pole straps tightened. Their quarters swung outwards as their inside hocks pushed against the front of the carriage which did not move backwards. I had proved my point and the driver agreed. It was not long before breechings and false martingales were added to this harness and the ponies were a lot happier.

In America, yoke harness is commonly seen on pairs put to light four wheelers such as buggies, buckboards and phaetons. Many of these vehicles have a pole which needs holding up at the collar end. The pole that is used with a British or European four-wheeled carriage is usually held in the fore carriage, where it slots into position at the turntable, being secured by a pole pin. However, many American vehicles are constructed on an entirely different design. The pole is made complete with a splinter bar which, in turn, holds each horse's whipple tree to take the traces. Curving down from the splinter bar are arms with fittings at their ends, which slot into receiving fittings by the front axle. The wood is curved and reinforced with metal at the stress points. The pole is held up by a leather fitting which is fixed to the centre of the yoke. The yoke, in turn, is held up by yoke straps which pass round the yoke, through dees, and are fixed around the base of each horse's collar. As the pole is very light, the weight is negligible.

Pairs are occasionally put to two wheelers, such as curricles, in which case curricle harness and a curricle bar are used. With this, the weight of the unbalanced vehicle, before the driver, passenger and rear-seated groom have mounted, is taken through the curricle bar, which lies through sideways terrets on the heavily padded saddles.

Belly bugle harness is sometimes used with Friesians put to a Friesian chaise. Here, the shaped metal bar, called a belly bugle, passes under both horses' bellies, being fixed to both horses' pads. There is loop in the bar in which the pole lies. It is very rare in Great Britain but I have seen it used in America with Friesian horses and, of course, it is used in the Netherlands.

Cape harness is used by a few people as a means of putting a pair in breast collar harness to a two wheeler. For this, a yoke is used which is held up by straps going over the ponies' necks. The straps are clipped at each end of the yoke, which is fixed to the pole with a specially shaped piece of strong leather.

The judge of pairs needs to be conversant with all of the types of harness he or she may meet when judging an open class.

If the turnout is formal, then it is quite correct for the driver to wear a top hat with his suit. The groom with such an equipage looks smartest in livery with a top hat, livery coat, white breeches and black boots with mahogany tops. A neatly tied stock should be worn with a plain pin. The groom should not wear a button-hole, although his master may wish to. Both should wear leather gloves, although string or wool is permissible if the weather is wet. It is important for hair to be tidy and for hats to be worn at the correct angle. Nothing looks worse than long hair hanging down below a top hat worn either on the back of the head or at a rakish angle.

A groom standing at the horses' heads should not hold them by the bars of their Buxton bits. These dressy bits have bars to prevent the coupling reins from getting caught in the cheeks and are not there for grooms to swing on. Any necessary handling should be done with the reins or the nosebands. When the groom mounts, he should do so neatly and smartly. He should sit as an upright figure with his knees together. Nothing looks worse than a groom sitting in a slovenly manner, with his legs apart, on the rear seat of a carriage. The groom does not wear an apron.

Any social passenger should wear an apron or have a rug to protect his or her clothes. Such a person should dress carefully so that the colouring of the dress does not clash with that of the Whip. Some competitors take great pains to have their female passenger on the box in a hat that complements the colouring of the carriage. This attention to detail makes a good first impression with the judge. Passengers who have not taken any trouble with the colour co-ordination of their clothing can spoil the overall picture. Too many passengers seated in a carriage can do the same thing. Sometimes, with a vehicle that has accommodation for a larger number of people, it can appear as though the whole family is on board for the outing. This is fine if that is what the driver wants to do but, when it comes to top class showing in a strong class of immaculate turnouts, the vehicle can look horribly overcrowded.

23 · TANDEMS

With over 160 tandem drivers now eligible to wear their 'tandem bars', as members of the Tandem Club of Great Britain, which I started with Lady Cromwell in 1977, the number of tandems being shown has increased considerably.

It used not to be necessary to have two animals which matched for height or colour in order to win in the show ring. Of course, in the seventies, there were a few lovely tandems made up with matching animals driven by great experts in the handling of these equipages and these stood deservedly at the top of the line in their classes. However, at that time I had a tandem which was made up with a 14.3 h.h. grey and a 13.3 h.h. dun and we won on quite a few occasions. We would definitely not be as successful now.

In a specialist class there will almost certainly be a number of top class tandems which will combine matching colour and height of animals with a good performance resulting from correct

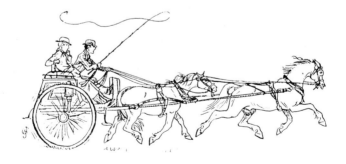

Figure 5 Tandem with a wheeler on tow.

production and schooling. A tandem, however, does not have to match for colour in the way that a pair does. For instance, a bay of a lighter build could look very smart in the lead of a tandem that has a bay and white skewbald wheeler of a slightly stockier frame. There are really no hard and fast rules because it will all be decided by the judge's personal preference. A lot will depend on the degree of training of the animals and on how well they are driven. The judge will be watching to see that they go one behind the other all the time. When they are coming directly towards the judge, the turnout should, ideally, look like a single. This is difficult to maintain and takes a lot of skill on the part of the driver. The greatest compliment that I can ever be given by a casual observer, whom I might meet when out driving, is for them to say something like, 'Oh! You've got two ponies. I thought when I first saw you coming down the road that you were only driving one.'

24　Cynthia Sheerman with Nork Gold Dust and Glanarthen Glyndwr to a dog cart, winners of their class for three consecutive years at the BDS Show.

There is often a misconception, when tandems are being driven in the show ring, that the leader's traces should be tight to prove that the leader is working. Commentators frequently give out, over the loud speaker, remarks that are intended to be knowledgeable, to the effect that the leader is not working, inferring that it should be. This makes the judge look very stupid when he pins the tricolour to such a tandem. So often, I have been told that people in the grandstand are overheard saying things like, 'The tandem isn't any good, the leader isn't working.' Because I am aware of this, I sometimes ask the commentator to explain that the leader is there to be called on, if necessary, to help to haul the load up hills or through deep going but that, on a level showground with a surface like a bowling green, it is the skill of the driver that is keeping the leader out of draught so that the traces swing gently, being looser than the reins.

The leader can be harnessed in a breast collar and the wheeler in a full collar if wished. When he executes his close inspection, the judge will be looking for such details as martingale-type trace carriers and crupper on the leader as well as all the necessary additions to the harness such as a bar bit on the wheeler, spring cock-eyes on the leader's traces and a safe means of fixing these to the wheeler's hame tug buckle.

On one occasion in America, a tandem of middleweight-type hunters came before me in their specialist class. The horses were superb and went extremely well. The harness, from a distance, looked equally good. On close inspection, however, I discovered that, instead of having steel spring cock-eyes at the ends of the traces, there were little solid brass hooks of the kind that might be found on a dog's lead. These were fixed to solid brass rings attached by leather and some stitching to the hame tugs on the wheeler. I mentioned to the driver that I was concerned about the safety of this arrangement, saying something to the effect that if and when she were to put her leader into draught, I suspected that either the hook would break or the stitching would tear. To my surprise she replied, 'Oh yes, it always does, what should I do?' I explained about such things as steel cock-eyes for the trace ends and steel connectors for the hame tug buckles. These were soon ordered and she was grateful that her problem had been solved.

The vehicle should, of course, be of adequate height for the driver to be able to see well over the top of both horses and the judge will take this into consideration. A carriage such as a high dog cart or cocking cart is ideal.

The usual appointments, such as the lamps and perhaps a dash board watch and horn case, will be seen, as will the spares kit which should contain a lead and wheel trace, lead and wheel rein and a hame strap if a full collar is worn as well as the usual knife and piece of cord. It is essential that a whip which is long enough to reach the leader is carried. A tandem leader can come round and face his driver as quickly as lightning can flash, so it is essential to be able to use the whip in order to prevent such an occurrence. Whereas team leaders have to hold a committee meeting before they can both decide to turn and face their driver, a tandem leader does not have to ask another horse. He just makes an instantaneous decision and, before his driver knows what is happening, the leader is coming round past the vehicle which is now turning and going back in the direction from which it has just come. It is for this reason that the driver must be skilful in both using and folding his tandem whip. The catching of a double thong is difficult and some drivers are tempted to secure their thong at the top of the whip with a piece of cotton wound round at the base where the goose quill is fixed by black thread to the stick. The thong then hangs neatly in the desired loop, which enables the wheeler to be hit. However, with the thong secured in this way, it cannot be unfolded to be applied to the leader. Such practice is both dangerous and foolish and the judge is unlikely to be taken in. It is far better to spend the time that it takes learning how to catch a thong so that it is there to be used if needed.

Some drivers wind the thong of their whip round the stick so many times that it is impossible to unfold it quickly enough to be applied in time. They twist it round the stick by hanging the whip over the edge of the vehicle and swinging the thong round and round until it is wrapped round the stick. This method is known as 'stirring whitewash' and is not to be recommended.

During the individual show, the judge will be watching to make sure the horses go correctly, one behind the other, at all times. During turns or figures, the wheeler must track behind the leader and not fall in on the bends. The halt must be square and the rein back straight. All that has been said regarding correct paces and outline applies to tandems just as much as to any other private driving turnout.

24 · RANDEMS

The class for randems (three in a row) was originally thought up by Richard James, director of the British Driving Society's Annual Show. The horses are put to as for tandem with an extra horse in front. The harness is similar to that used with a tandem but has one more leader set. Some competitors use two sides of a set of pair harness for the leader and swing (centre) horse, with long traces, additional pad and bridle terrets and very long leader reins.

Six reins are held in the hand in the same principle as four with team and tandem. The judging of the class is mainly on the driver's ability to handle the randem but, of course, correct turnout is important. Competitors are required to trot a figure of eight during their individual show. The need to have onward-going horses can create a problem in that care has to be taken that the leader and/or the swing horse does not get into more draught than the shaft horse and create a tug of war in which the wheeler can get pulled off his feet. Also, if the leader or swing horse is in draught and the wheeler is not, then, because he is being towed along, the steering is lost. It is unlikely that the leader can be reached with the whip, so he has to be forward going. An animal which is the distance away from the driver that is necessary with a randem leader has to have a lot of courage to perform that job all by himself. Such horses are not easy to find.

With the ideal randem, all three horses will match for colour, type and way of going. The harness will also match, whether it is two sides of a pair or two tandem leader sets with a wheeler set of the same pattern. The vehicle must be of a suitable fit, height and type for a randem. One which is low will not be easy for the driver. A two wheeler is preferable to a four-wheeled

25 Bill Vine driving his randem of Welsh cross Irish Draught horses to a tandem club cart to win his class and the BDS show championship.

vehicle. The Whip has to be a master in the art of handling six reins in order to win the class and he will have to get full co-operation from all three horses during the time that he is in the ring being judged. It is essential to have highly trained, free-moving and sensible horses and a groom who is athletic and quick thinking.

25 · THE COACHING CLASS

The sight and sound of a team of four horses put to a coach draws spectators to the ringside like a magnet. Because of the space needed for such equipages, the preliminary judging frequently takes place in a designated area of the show ground where there is enough room for the teams to stand for the judge to inspect each turnout before they go on the drive. Small side rings do not usually allow enough space or have good enough access as the length of a coach and four is considerable. The equipage is not anything like as manoeuvrable as a team put to one of the modern four wheelers used for horse driving trials, which can be spun round with one rear wheel pivoting as the front wheels turn right underneath the body of the vehicle.

The judge will be taken to the preliminary judging area by his steward and will walk from one coach and four to another in order to inspect every exhibit closely.

The coaching class is sometimes divided into three sections and this has to be remembered when the preliminary inspection is taking place. One section could be for private coaches, also known as drags or park drags. Another section could be for regimental coaches, which are drags owned by a regiment. The third section could be for road coaches.

Because of the manner in which the teams are often forced to assemble in a given area, I always ask the coachman on the box if he is ready to have his equipage judged before I begin my inspection. There is so much to be considered when judging coaching that I feel it unfair to start judging one person when others are having extra time to deal with last-minute details. So, if a driver says that he is not quite ready for me to start judging his coach, I go on to another team whose driver is ready and

26 Anne and Peter Munt with their Gelderlander team to a park drag, winning the coaching class at the Suffolk County Show in 1993.

will be pleased for me to get this inspection done.

Of course, none of this applies if the preliminary judging is executed in an arena where the usual judging procedure takes place. Teams are seen working in both directions and are then lined up for detailed inspection before going out on their road drive which, in coaching, is still called a marathon. It is usually in the region of between 8 and 13 km (5–8 miles) along roads and, if the country permits, tracks. Teams are not asked to go across rough country.

This drive is similar to that for the private driving classes. The judge is taken to certain points in a car by his steward so that he can see how each team performs on the road. It is advantageous to see the horses going up and down hills, as well as round a corner, if this can be arranged. Discussion with the car driver beforehand gives him time to think of the best way to go to take his judge to the most advantageous viewing points. It can be difficult if the car driver has to overtake a long convoy of coaches, so he needs time to work out how he can take a short cut to come out in front of the teams at a point further along the route.

The way in which the horses work as a team will be particularly noted. The most common fault with newcomers to this aspect of driving is that they allow their leaders to do more work than their wheelers. The wheelers' traces will be seen to be slack and the leaders' traces will be taut. This is an extremely bad state of affairs which can lead to all kinds of problems. It is particularly dangerous in going down a hill, when the wheelers could get pulled off their feet. The leaders must be seen to be kept out of draught when the team is going down a hill and they must be well into draught, as must the wheelers, when ascending a gradient. The problem that some people experience in allowing their leaders to do more work than their wheelers usually occurs because the horses chosen as the leaders are naturally very onward going and tend to pull their reins through their driver's fingers, a little at a time, without him realizing. The driver must keep a close watch on the rein splices in front of his hands. If the splices move a fraction further away, he should be warned that the reins are slipping, even if he thinks that they are not. Of course, experienced team drivers are fully aware of the potential problem and do not allow their reins to slip through their fingers.

Whether put to a road coach or a private coach, the teams should work well together and have a good outline. The overall appearance will be ruined if one animal is perpetually breaking pace into a canter, star gazing, or hanging back behind his collar with his nose stuck out. So often in a team there is one that is either hot-headed or idle, which ruins the overall impression for the judge. Sometimes there is one which is a worrier or a bad traveller in a horse box, so he always appears to be tucked up and looks thin compared with the other three. It is extremely difficult to find four horses of the type needed for coaching. It is permissible to have slightly larger horses in the wheel.

Keeping sixteen legs free from knocks is not easy and the judge will be looking around the limbs for lumps, bumps and such things as brushing marks. Sixteen feet and sets of shoes, in good condition, is another very important point at which the judge will be looking. One horse with bad feet in a team affects the reliability of the whole turnout as he is quite likely to shed a shoe at any time, even if he has been recently and properly

27 George Mossman driving the *Bedford Times* coach, frequent winners of road coach classes.

shod. Animals with feet like colanders will be noticed by the judge and placed accordingly. It all comes back to the saying, 'No foot, no horse' which probably applies to coaching more than any other equine sport.

The horses used in a road coach need to be strong enough to pull the vehicle which is likely to be heavier than a private coach. They do not necessarily have to match in colour. It is quite permissible to have a coloured horse in the off lead. It is also acceptable to have a cross or chequer board team with two greys and two bays, browns or blacks. This was sometimes favoured when road coaches worked a century ago, as the contrasting colours helped the team to show up on a dark night to other road users. Horses that are put to a drag are best if they match for colour. They should be of good breeding yet have substance. They must be full of presence and have showy action which matches for stride but they should not be too flashy. Their manners must be perfect for their owner to drive. In the past, white markings were not considered desirable but now numerous teams of Gelderlanders with white legs are put to private coaches and these have become acceptable and look very smart indeed. They have a proud way of going and look extremely well in the coaches to which they are put.

The harness which is used with a private coach is lighter than that for a road coach. Similar comparisons apply as with private driving harness and that which is used with trade turnouts. Drag harness is of double-stitched black leather with patent on such places as the collars, pads, blinkers, face drops and false martingale fronts. Such niceties as three rivets on the hame clips and martingale-type cruppers are advantageous. Buxton bits are used. Some people add bearing reins, in which case they should be on all four horses. With a road coach, Liverpool bits or elbow bits with bars are used and a bearing rein can be put on to one horse only, if desired. Road coach harness is heavier and tougher. It was originally made this way so that it would withstand all the rigours of daily use in all weathers on the coaching runs. Polished brown leather collars are worn, with the rest of the harness being of black leather. A spare collar, made of rush, generally known as a straw collar, is sometimes hung on the side of a road coach. Connecting straps, which are now often used between the collars of horse driving trials teams, are not used with coaching teams. The hames used with a road coach team have ring draught at the traces which have loops at their ends. Drag harness traces have quick-release ends or loops. The browbands on road coach harness are often of metal or metal and leather to match the colour of the coach. The initial letters of the name of the coach, such as RR for Red Rover, decorates such places as the blinkers and pads. Drag harness is decorated with the owner's crest or monogram as are the crest panel and hind boot of the coach. The vehicle is often painted in the family's colours. A drag is usually built to a more refined finish than a road coach. It might have such niceties as discreet carving on the undercarriage, whereas the splinter bar and futchells of a road coach would probably be plain. The road coach has a net of leather straps for coats and light pieces of luggage between the roof seats whose lazy backs are permanently up. The drag has lazy backs which are hinged down when passengers are not carried. There is sometimes an imperial (picnic box) between these seats.

Whether the furniture on the harness, the metal on the coach and the buttons on the grooms' livery coats are of brass or silver plate can depend on whether the family colours include yellow or white. The judge will be looking for matching-coloured metal throughout the turnout.

The road coach will be painted more brightly than the drag and will have the names of some of the places at which it stops along its route. For instance, the Red Rover has London, Southampton and The Bull, East Sheen, written on it, which are all on the route that it ran over a century ago. The name of the coach will be painted on the back panel. The hind boot is designed so that it opens on the left, being hinged on the right. The scarlet-coated guard will sit on the left of the rear seat so that he is able to reach down to open the boot. He will wear a leather pouch containing an open-faced watch (the judge may check the time on this) and a key which opens the boot. The judge will certainly ask for the boot to be opened so that he can inspect the spares which are carried. The boot of a private coach hinges at the bottom to form a tray so that, when the groom opens the boot, the judge is able to see how this is fitted out. Some have splendid zinc-lined wine racks and food containers for the picnic. In a private coach, such things as spares, headcollars and rugs for the horses are carried in the front boot. The lamps are usually hung up in holders in the interior of the coach which will have a superior trim to that of the inside of a road coach.

The two grooms are carried on rumble seats on iron stays with a drag, whereas the rear seat of a road coach can accommodate three passengers alongside the guard. Attention to the way in which the grooms mount is important. When the coach is stationary, one will be at the heads of the leaders and the other will stand by the wheelers. A nod from the driver should result in them both stepping aside as the team walks forward. The groom who was at the front walks towards the rear of the coach and the other groom pauses for a moment. Then, as the drag passes the grooms, they are in position to be able to walk in step. As the rear of the coach comes alongside the grooms, they both mount in unison and reach their respective seats to sit down at the same time. This needs a lot of careful practice but, once perfected, it adds to the neatness of their mounting and shows the judge that attention has been paid to yet another detail of the presentation of the turnout.

When the coaches return from the marathon, no rubbing down is permitted until the judge has completed his inspection of all the exhibits and given his permission. The coaches are then brought into the main ring for the final judging. They are driven round, first in one direction and then in the other, before being lined up, in their sections, in order of placing. Sometimes, the show organizers like to keep the coaches in the ring for quite a long time so that the spectators have plenty of opportunity to see them. The judge may then ask each team to go out and give an individual display. It is up to the coachman to do whatever he chooses. The judge will make his final decision regarding the placings after he has seen all the displays. In Great Britain it is not usual to ask the coachmen to rein back their teams. However, a few occasionally choose to back their coach to show how well trained their animals are. It is very difficult for a coaching team to back, as breechings are not usually worn and the horses have to push the coach back by taking the weight entirely on the tops of their collars against their necks.

Before the awards are presented, if the class has been divided into various sections it is important to tell the steward to advise the commentator of the divisions so that the spectators can be kept informed. Otherwise, the results can appear rather bewildering to people at the ringside.

Sometimes there is an award for the best performance on the coach horn. If a horn blower is carried on the coach, he will usually blow his horn whenever he sees the judge on the marathon in order to demonstrate his skills. The blowing is often far better on the road, when the coach is running along a smooth surface, than it is when they get back into the ring where it can be much harder to keep the horn steady against the lips while the coach is bumping about on the grassy terrain. The decision on the award for the best horn blower should, therefore, not depend entirely on the performance heard in the arena. Some horn blowers may play five notes when out on the road, while others may only manage to get one or two clean notes from their horn. At some shows, the horn blowing prize is judged by an independent person in the grandstand, in which case, of course, the decision rests entirely on the performance given in the arena when the coaches are being finally judged. The horn blower then demonstrates his skills when the coachman takes his equipage out to give his individual show. In this way, each musician can be heard and assessed. In these circumstances, the judge of the horn blowing must judge what he hears and not what someone tells him he would have heard if he had been out on the road with the coaching judge.

The passengers carried on a coach need to be briefed regarding their dress, as in any other showing class. Clashing colours will detract from the overall impression given to the judge, as will overcrowding by having too many people on the coach. There should, however, be a minimum of six people carried, including the coachman.

26 · THE TEAM CLASS

At some shows there are classes for competitors who have a team of horses or ponies which they drive to a vehicle such as a brake, dog cart or wagonette.

The judge will be looking for animals that are suitable for the vehicle to which they are put and for the harness and appointments to be appropriate. If, for instance, there is a team of Shetland ponies in brown harness, put to a varnished wagonette, then the grooms should be of suitable size for the vehicle and should be dressed in country clothes which complement the turnout. They would be incorrect in full livery. The ponies should be seen to match in their stride and way of going, with all four working together as required. It is a common fault among newcomers to driving teams to have the leaders in draught more than the wheelers. The judge will be watching for such errors of coachmanship. He will probably mention this to the driver when the opportunity arises during the presentation of awards. Another common fault is for the driver, when progressing from halt to walk, to allow his leaders to step forward

Figure 6   An ill-matched team.

fractionally before his wheelers. He should start the vehicle moving with the wheelers slightly before the leaders.

Some teams are made up of two obvious pairs instead of four matching animals and this does not present a good picture.

Another fault is for the vehicle to be overhorsed. This probably stems from horse driving trials when small, close-coupled vehicles, which are easier to get through tight places in the obstacles on a marathon during the cross country phase, are put behind big horses. Although this is necessary for eventing, the overall picture is not as pleasing to the judge's eye in a showing class, as one in which the horses and vehicle are in proportion. As in any other form of showing, it is important to have horses or ponies who are correctly and carefully schooled. They will then be likely to carry their heads at matching angles and work stride for stride, which gives a superb overall picture. They need to be schooled individually, on the principles of ridden dressage, so that when they are put into the team they will go with the same outline. Such animals will then work with ease and efficiency and take far less out of themselves than animals who are not happy in their mouths through lack of schooling before they are

28 Peter and Joan Clarke with their team of prize-winning Welsh ponies to a dog cart.

put together as a team. If one is a star gazer and one is overbent, another pokes its nose out and the fourth carries its head low, however well they match for colour and however much everything is highly polished and newly painted, if the overall outline is not pleasing then, when it comes to the awards, the final placing can never be high. The judge will almost certainly choose a team which he thinks would give him pleasure to drive. He is unlikely to pick a team as his winner, which appears to be creating problems for its driver.

The same remarks apply to the judging of a unicorn team (two wheelers and one leader) which is sometimes judged in the class with the four-in-hands.

27 · HORSE DRIVING TRIALS

Judges at horse driving trials need to have exceptionally good memories in order to be conversant with all the rules that apply to the three phases of an event. A copy of the rule book, with all the amendments added, must be kept close to hand at all times.

It is a great help to have competed in this aspect of the sport of carriage driving before serving the probationary period needed to become a judge. In fact, most new judges either are, or have been, competitors in driving trials. Probationer judges are trained by experienced judges before being put on to the List Three Panel once they are considered to be proficient. They are then only allowed to judge singles and pairs, in the company of a List One or Two judge at national level. They often gain experience at club level where they are likely to judge allcomers. After serving enough time on List Three, they may be upgraded to List Two. List One judges are those who are selected to judge at international driving trials. For this, it is a help to be able to speak such languages as French and German. These panels of judges consist of people who have the necessary experience to judge the cones competition, deal with queries regarding the marathon and have the required depth of knowledge to judge the dressage phase.

Obstacle stewards on the cross country phase do not have to be on the judges' panel. Their job is simply to observe and record the routes and behaviour of each competitor as they drive through the obstacle at which they are positioned, so that faults are recorded. Panel judges are placed to check competitors at the start and finish of the marathon in order to deal with queries. They are also present at the compulsory halts at the end

29 Gay and Tony Russell with Formakin Merlyn to a Genesis competition vehicle, on their way to winning the dressage phase and the single horse class at Thoresby Park Driving Trials in 1993.

of the walk sections when a decision may have to be made, in conjunction with the duty veterinary surgeon, as to whether a horse or pony is considered to be unfit to continue.

In order to judge the dressage phase, it is essential to be fully conversant with the test in question. It is a help to have driven the test at home a few times before judging as likely problems are then fully appreciated. For this reason, I also find it useful to have taught pupils to drive the particular test because then, even more, the difficulties which may arise with competitors do not come as a surprise.

It has to be remembered that dressage is a thing of beauty and elegance and the test should be a happy occasion for all concerned. With careful training, a very ordinary animal can become beautiful because of its correct, confident and obedient way of going. The test should be a pleasure for the judge to watch, not an endurance test because it is so bad. It should be smooth and accurate, being executed with calmness, and yet full of impulsion, with plenty of energy coming from the hind quarters. The paces must be true and correct. The outline should be pleasing, with no tendency to be stiff, hollow or overbent. The horse must accept the bit with a light contact on his driver's hands and bend in the direction of the movement. If a multiple is being driven, then they must be working as one, not as separate animals.

It is essential to set a standard to which all marks from ten to nought will relate. When giving marks, it is important to dictate as many comments as possible to the writer. These are a great help, both to the competitor, when he receives his dressage sheet, and to the judge if confronted by the competitor a week or so later, over the telephone. If this should happen, the written remarks will bring back the whole picture to the judge who will then be able to explain, more fully, his reasons for the particular mark which is causing concern.

There was one particular occasion when I had slaughtered a competitor with twos, threes and fours on their sheet for an appalling test with a pair. I happened to be at the start of the marathon the following day and received some not very polite remarks about my judging from this competitor. I agreed to meet her later, at the end of the day, when we had both finished, in order to go right through her sheet. We spent a very constructive hour or so together and parted amicably after I had been able to explain my reasoning. She went away happily, agreeing that her pair needed a lot of work and that they had been hurried too much in order to compete at this particular event. She promised that she would work them carefully in the way in which I suggested. I saw them again the following year, greatly improved. If I had not dictated long remarks to my scribe after each mark, I doubt very much if I would have been able to remember exactly how those animals had gone.

A driven dressage judge is sometimes expected to judge for up to eight hours and, on one occasion, I judged for nearly nine. With different classes, ranging from singles, through pairs or tandems perhaps to pony and/or horse teams, it would be quite impossible to remember a particular performance in detail without written comments as a reminder. However familiar a competitor may be to the judge, he must judge what he sees. A previous performance must not relate to the performance that is being driven at the time of judging. Some judges can be disappointed by what they see from a particular competitor, so they mark this person too low. Sometimes, if several bad tests have been seen and then someone comes in and drives a relatively good test, the relief at seeing a reasonable test can result in marks which are perhaps too generous.

I never give a nought as I always think that something has been performed providing that the turnout remains in the arena. Of course, if it leaves the arena, the competitor is eliminated. In the final analysis the judge will ask himself if the test was pleasant to watch. Horses which are trained correctly are likely to execute a pleasing test. There is only one way to get good dressage marks and that is to spend time on training so that the animal understands what is required.

At national competitions, the dressage judges are positioned at C, B and E, with the most senior adjudicator at C. This judge is responsible for stopping the competitor if he makes an error of course. Marks for this are deducted from his score sheet. The other judges should write a remark about the error on their sheet and mark the movement accordingly when it is performed. It also falls on the shoulders of the judge at C to make decisions regarding marked lameness and such matters as grooms dismounting or prompting the driver or for elimination due to the turnout leaving the arena.

At club events, there may be either one or two judges by the dressage arena. One is always at C and if there is a second judge they can sit either at B or at E. Very often the choice will be made according to the direction of the sun's rays. Sitting for hours inside a hot car, on a chair outside the car or even at a table under a sun shade facing the sun is very tiring. Sometimes the judges at E and B share the punishment of the sun as they mutually agree to change places between classes. Obviously, a judge cannot change position during a class. A driving dressage judge looks for many of the same things as a ridden dressage judge. The main differences are that in driven dressage the use of the voice is permitted and the driven horse has to maintain its balance and correct way of going at the same time as pulling a cart, which makes it more difficult to achieve the same high standard that good ridden dressage horses obtain. Of course, the driven horse does not have to execute any canter or lateral work, neither is he asked to show collected or extended walk. He is, however, expected to move with good rhythm, have correct, regular paces and be obedient at all times.

There are no mysteries to dressage. The horse must be well schooled. The most common fault, when starting the test, is for the turnout to take a wavering line instead of a straight entry. This is usually caused by overcorrection on the part of the driver, instead of keeping a steady hand with the horse going forward on to the bit. The judge at C will notice the crooked line much more than the judges at E and B who will not be able to see this so clearly unless it is very pronounced. They will, however, be able to see the accuracy of the position of the halt at X, while the judge at C may find this harder to observe. Many harness horses step back when they halt, in order to relieve the pressure on their collars. This is a bad fault and costs marks. It takes considerable training to teach the horse to go forward into a square halt and hold the position with its weight evenly distributed over all four legs and with a steady head and not to step back while his driver salutes. This is more difficult for a man as, in order to take off his hat, he has to place his reins and whip in his left hand in order to free his right hand to remove his head gear. For this manoeuvre to be executed neatly and without hurry, the horse must maintain the halt for several seconds. It is a common fault for the salute to be hurried and given almost before the halt has been properly established.

On moving forward, the transition must be smooth and calm, yet onward going. There must be no tendency to jerkiness which, again, particularly among novices, is a common fault. The first turn should be made after going through the centre of G towards C. Again, novices tend to start turning to M or H at G. It must be remembered that a quarter of a circle should be driven at each corner. The words 'full use not made of arena' are often written on the score sheet for this reason. Drivers make the test so much more difficult for themselves if they keep cutting across the arena at every corner. Such a movement as an extended trot across the diagonal from M to K through X is so much more difficult if the turn to M has been cut short, so that the horse arrives well away from the boards at M, is forced to turn short and is therefore well on the way to X before he is able to lengthen his stride. It is, of course, essential that the rhythm remains the same through collected, working and extended trots and that the stride is shortened and lengthened as desired. The judges will be watching for such faults as hurried paces and loss of rhythm in the extended trot. So many horses and ponies are hurried by their drivers instead of lengthened. The stride should be stretched into extension and shortened for collection.

The walk causes problems for some competitors. Judges are looking for a regular and active four-time beat. So often the beat is hurried, with the horse moving in a stride which inclines towards lateral two time.

The rein back should be in diagonal two time. This is a difficult movement for a harness horse to execute correctly, in that pushing a vehicle backwards, sometimes through heavy going, is not easy. This particularly applies to four-wheeled carriages. The front wheel only has to hit a small rut or stone in order to cause the vehicle to jack-knife, thus gaining the remark on the sheet of 'crooked rein back'.

Circles can create quite a lot of problems for competitors. Very often a horse falls in towards the centre and the driver has to try to keep him out with the whip. If this fails then sometimes the outer rein is used, which causes the horse to bend away from the direction of the movement. The judge's remark may then be to the effect that the bend is wrong and the horse is looking out of the circle. It has to be remembered that circles should be round. So often, the first half is driven correctly and the second half is driven flat. Work under saddle is needed, so that the rider's legs can be used to train most horses to execute good circles. In the case of two half-circles being driven, say BX half-circle right, XE half-circle left, the judge will be watching for the correct bend to the right then for the horse to be straightened momentarily as he goes through X before bending correctly to the left between X and E. The different judges at the side and at C will all see different things through this movement. It is for this reason that competitors, on receiving their score sheets, will sometimes find that the marks given by the judges vary considerably. This is because one judge is almost sure to see things which another judge is unable to see from his particular position at the side of the arena, and vice versa. It all usually levels out in the end.

In Advanced tests, there are sometimes movements which have to be driven with the reins in one hand and the whip held out to the right side so that the judges can see from a distance that that hand is not on the reins. It is important that competitors read the test sheet carefully because it is not unknown for them to misunderstand what is required and to bring their right hand back too soon, for which they then get marked down.

It is usually found that drivers who enter at A with their reins held in two, separated hands, that is with the left rein (or reins in the case of a team or tandem) in the left hand and the right rein, or reins, held in the right hand, get into a muddle when it comes to any of the movements which require the reins to be held in the left hand. They very often just appear to thrust the reins into a single hand and hope for the best. Usually, at about halfway through the movement, the bewildered horse, or horses, goes off course and the right hand is then brought back in order to sort out the problem. A low mark is sure to be given by all three judges for 'second hand came back early' as all will certainly have been able to see this mistake.

The final halt is as important as the first. Many novice drivers are so relieved that they have finished the test that they cannot wait to get out of the arena. The result is that the salute is sometimes given before the halt is established. From a judge's point of view, it is nice to receive a smile from the competitor as the salute is given, as a way of saying 'thank you for judging me'. In the same vein, when leaving the arena, it is appreciated if the competitor gives a nod or passing salute and smile to the judges at B and E as he drives towards the exit at A. The concentration required to enable the judge to remain consistent throughout a long class is considerable and the occasional smile is much appreciated.

There are no short cuts to training horses correctly and far too many people are in too much of a hurry to compete with young horses which are neither mentally nor physically capable of coping with the stress and strain of high-level horse driving trials. Training takes a very long time and the final result of careful education is far superior to that of a horse which is hurried and not given sufficient time to mature before the big questions are asked. An animal who has been brought on slowly and properly prepared is far more likely to last for several years and to stay sound than one that has been pushed too soon and probably ends up with mouth, back and mental problems from which he may never fully recover.

Horses and ponies that have been schooled under saddle and on long reins are likely to be the ones who will gain the highest marks on the judges' sheets in the dressage phase. Their high degree of training will also make them far more manoeuvrable through cross country obstacles and when it comes to the cones course.

Many years ago, I was invited and I accepted to judge at a driving trials in a country which had better remain unnamed. My knowledge of the language spoken was limited to what I had learned at school, which I had mostly forgotten. I had a miserable time because, as a dressage judge, all the important things I needed to say had lost their impact by the time they had been related to the president of the jury at C by my writer who was bilingual. As I positioned myself at E, I noticed that the competitors would not be able to enter at A because there was a hedge partly in the way. I was told that this did not matter. They were all going to enter the arena at the side of C and come round inside and then turn down the centre as near to A as well as they could. Naturally, I found this hard to accept and, as predicted, this was bad enough for the singles but made life very difficult for the pairs. Luckily there were no teams or tandems at that time. Then, I noticed that, although the letters R and P were in position, S and V were missing. Again I sent a message through my interpreter but this had no impact and all the tests were driven with these two letters missing. A third problem arose when one of the competitors took the wrong course. They were not stopped and the resulting test had movements being executed in the wrong places. I was becoming frantic. It was impossible to judge the dressage at the same time as trying to attract the eye of the judge at C, who appeared to be quite oblivious of the error as the situation got worse and worse. When the competitor finally left the arena, I was certain that we would be called to discuss the situation. My hopes were shattered when, within a few moments, the next competitor came in to be judged. I often wonder what my writer put on the sheet when all I kept saying was 'error of course' and 'circle in the wrong place', and tried to mark movements which were being driven in the wrong places with more comments of 'course error'. I wonder what the scorers did. No one ever asked me. After the class was over, I queried this particular competitor's test and was met with a blank expression from the judge at C. I vowed that I would never, ever again accept an invitation to judge in a country where I am unable to converse competently. Amazingly, I was invited to go back another year to judge the dressage at the same event but I refused because I really could

30 Mark Gaskin driving his horses in a cones competition to win the pairs class.

not face such frustration again. A judge needs to communicate!

Panel judges are also expected to judge the cones phase at a horse driving trials. This is not always problem-free and can sometimes demand a lot of mental agility. It is important to walk and learn the course before judging. Great concentration is needed. The course plan and the rule book need to be close to hand. Things happen very quickly and decisions have to be made instantly regarding such matters as an error of course. Another thing which can make judging this phase difficult is that the judge's ears have to be shut to all the communications which are often coming over the telephone placed in the judges' box by the side of the arena. While having to make vital and instant decisions about such things as ringing the bell to stop the competitor, there may be queries being discussed by others in the box about the timing of the presentation of awards to another class or someone who has now been found to have been eliminated in the marathon which is causing their running order to be changed. The steward concerned has to be notified. There is never a dull moment. A horse driving trials judge's job is not an easy one and must not be undertaken lightly.

28 · CONCLUSION

There are occasions when a judge is faced with problems before, during or after judging which relate to the organization of the classes or the administration of the show. Usually, there is nothing that can be done on the day, either to alter the facilities that have been made available or to change the planning of the classes. All that the judge can do is smile and get on with the job of judging. It is no good storming into the secretary's tent and expecting something to be done. Everyone will be far too busy to pay much attention.

Sometimes the actual show ring leaves a lot to be desired. At a county show, or large show of that standard, the ring is likely to be as near to excellence as possible. It will probably have been cared for by a team of people whose knowledge of grassland management has been put into practice throughout the period from the previous year's show to the current occasion. However, at a small show it may be discovered that the area which has been allocated for the driving classes is far from perfect. It may be on a slope, so that competitors are either going up a hill or down a hill during the entire time that they are in the ring. The area may be long and narrow to the point of being dangerous when all the competitors are in together. The surface may be covered with sheep or cattle manure because the stock which was put in at the last minute to graze the area down, had not been removed until the day before the show. The surface may be rough and have visible or invisible pot holes.

If the area is very bumpy, the judge should tell the steward to warn the competitors about the terrain and ask them to enter at the walk and remain at that gait until everyone has had a chance to see for themselves how their vehicle is coping with the bumps.

Such conditions can result in lamps jumping out of their holders and, in extreme cases, a driver or passenger could get pitched from their seat. Many years ago, I was thrown out of my gig when I hit an unseen pot hole in a show ring and woke up two days later in hospital! In such a ring, it might be wise to tell competitors that they may ask their grooms to remove the lamps from their vehicles once the initial inspection has been completed. A quiet word to the steward could be in order so that he can mention the views of the judge at the after-show stewards' inquest. This can be reinforced with a carefully worded letter to the show secretary, explaining the possible dangers of an unsuitable ring or a poor surface. When writing to the show organizers with any criticism, it is essential to word the letter tactfully. A letter must *never* be sent in anger as this is certain to do much more harm than good. Diplomacy is of paramount importance.

There are times when turnouts are forced to plough through deep mud in the ring if there has been a lot of rain and the driving classes have followed a display of tractors and heavy farm implements which have churned the surface into a morass. This can result in mud and grass hanging from the axles of the carriages, white socks which look brown and ends of tails hanging in balls of mud. All of this is heartbreaking for the competitors who have probably spent hours, days and weeks getting ready to produce immaculate turnouts. In such a case, a letter to the secretary would not go amiss, explaining how much the competitors suffered during their classes and how concerned everyone is about the plans for the following year's show.

There are times when the private driving class has been left open to allcomers of every possible shape and size, with no regard to the fact that there is likely to be a very large number of entries competing for a single set of rosettes and prizes. All that can usually be done on the day is for the judge to judge the class as it is stated in the schedule, where the prizes are probably being given to sixth place and rosettes to tenth. This, however, leaves too many disgruntled competitors. I had an instance of this at a very large show where I was faced with a huge mixed entry of all types and sizes. It was very unsatisfactory for all concerned. I wrote to the show secretary afterwards, stating my suggestions for four divisions and giving the exact wording. I was glad to see later that the committee obviously agreed because there are now four, properly divided classes and everyone is presumably a lot happier.

Sometimes, following correspondence between the show secretary and the judge after the invitation has been accepted, a copy of the previous year's show schedule is sent to enable the judge to see the classification. This gives the opportunity for any wording that may be questionable to be discussed and altered. On more than one occasion, I have written to the secretary suggesting a change in the wording, which has resulted in the classification being altered, for the better, for competitors.

There are times when an unsuitable route for the road drive has been chosen. I do not think it wise to take competitors along a classified A road. It only needs one animal or one impatient motorist to do something silly for there to be a major pile up. Lack of proper policing is also sometimes a worry. Civilians in show cars do not receive the same respect from motorists as members of the police force with flashing lights. I do not really approve of a convoy of turnouts being asked to go over a level crossing just in case one horse were to turn and go down the track. Unmade roads with stony surfaces are not suitable for private driving vehicles because of the possible damage to the wheels of these highly painted and expensive carriages. As it now costs thousands of pounds to restore a vehicle to show condition, competitors are not keen to get them scratched on the road drive.

Sometimes a steward is very inefficient about his job, greeting the judge with a remark such as, 'I've never done this before so you will have to bear with me' and then promptly disappears so that the judge becomes his own steward for the class. Another type of steward will have done the job for years and may be very keen to tell the judge exactly how the competitors, who are now in the ring, were placed last year. Such people must be politely, but firmly, told that this is of no consequence because, 'I don't want to know and I am judging what I see today.' For this very reason, I prefer not to be seen to be talking to my steward in the ring as it can look, from the grandstand, as if I am asking his opinion when, in fact, I might only be asking him how we are going for our timing. If I do have anything specific to say, I try to turn aside and speak without looking at him unless, of course, it is something like the order in which I want the competitors brought into the line up. I avoid calling anyone by a name and so would say, 'Grey first, top hat second'. If the steward replies with 'Bob first', I repeat 'Grey first', even if we all know the well-known character who is coming into line.

When the steward has taken down the results for the judge's book, which he is asked to sign, it is wise to check that the correct numbers have been noted. This is vital because the prize money will be sent to the competitors numbered and also the results will be published in the press. It is sensible to check this when the steward accompanies the judge to the outside of the ring after the class. At this point, a catalogue can be consulted to make certain that the correct numbers have been put down to tally with the names.

I have, on a rare occasion, had stewards who have enjoyed too good a lunch. All that can be done then is to handle the class without stewards who are unlikely to be paying much attention if they are too busy talking among themselves. Such an occurrence is best dealt with by means of a quiet word to someone in authority, as a letter could cause too much trouble.

The secretary of a large show usually asks for comments from the judge about the way in which their particular section was run when they write their 'thank you' letter. This gives a perfect opportunity for the judge to reply with any constructive ideas about possible improvements to the classes or administration in general. The reply will probably be read at the next meeting, enabling a full discussion with the show committee. A judge should write to the show secretary if he feels strongly about anything which needs altering to make the show more enjoyable for all concerned the following year. It is, however, very important to be positive and not abrasive when writing with suggestions. Ideas that could be misconstrued as personal criticism could result in getting everyone's back up and make the committee decide to scrap the driving class because 'these people are always grumbling'.

There is no doubt that judging carriage driving is fun. The competitors may get their prizes and rosettes but the judges get their badges. Viewing the collection of judge's badges which I have accumulated over nearly 30 years brings back many happy memories for me. Each badge tells a story.

INDEX

Page numbers in *italics* refer to illustrations

116